THE CURSE

A SHOCKING TRUE STORY OF SUPERSTITION, HUMAN SACRIFICE AND CANNIBALISM

RYAN GREEN

Disclaimer

This book is about real people committing real crimes. The story has been constructed by facts but some of the scenes, dialogue and characters have been fictionalised.

Polite Note to the Reader

This book is written in British English except where fidelity to other languages or accents are appropriate. Some words and phrases may differ from US English.

Copyright © Ryan Green 2019

CONTENTS

Wash Away Your Sins

Mama was acting strange. In itself, that wasn't so strange. Mama was always a little bit off-kilter, but this weird interlude still stood out from the crowd. It was hard to say exactly when Mama started acting strange because it had always been the background noise to their life together. Not a day went by that she didn't consult her cards or read her tea leaves before making a decision.

It was probably harder to see when the rest of the world was just as chaotic as the storm going on inside her head. When the earth was shaking, and they had to flee across country, all her talk of curses and magic seemed almost logical. It was hard to see the earth shudder and shuck you from your home without feeling like there were some dark forces at work.

Since they'd settled here and life had become more comfortable, Giuseppe had hoped that all of that would fade back into the background. It had not. If anything, access to a little bit of wealth had only exaggerated all of the problems, as though she'd always been waiting to blossom into this thing — this sideshow to the village. There wasn't a man or woman in town that didn't know his mother now, and none of them would have spoken about her fine sons or her soap shop in the first breath. There would've been stories about her reading their palms, warning them of dire omens, giving them the kind of spiritual guidance that the church would never dare. Among the young people of Correggio, there was an edge of humour about it. They rolled their eyes at their superstitious mothers asking advice from the fortune teller. Yet, none of them would stray from his mother's advice if she gave it. They doubted if her fortunes were true, but the old superstitions ran deep even now, and they wouldn't put themselves in harm's way just for the sake of proving her wrong.

That was the background strangeness that Giuseppe wouldn't have even remarked upon — the strange way that his mother lived on the periphery of society in town yet somehow managed to control so much of what went on. When he finally moved away, it was one of the many things that he was looking forward to never dealing with again.

He loved his mother, just as surely as he knew she loved him, but her certainty in the truth of her visions and premonitions made her difficult to live with. There would be days when he would walk past the soap shop and see that it was still shuttered at midday because Mama had a bad dream about something the night before and had to spend her day purifying herself in the woods. There would be nights when he stirred in his sleep to find her looming over him like the hag of the old wives' tales, muttering under her voice in languages that he couldn't understand. The first time he'd found a talisman under his pillow, made of bird bones and bright thread, he cast the thing out of his window in disgust, but now, he accepted such things as a part of her love for him. She saw the world through this lens, and these strange little gifts and blessings were her way of showing that she cared.

The only trouble was, Mama couldn't be reasoned with. Normally, that meant little things like only eating fish for supper on a certain day, or walking to work by a different route, and he went along with it, unquestioning. He may not have had his friends' cowed approach to his mother's proclamations, but where they might have obeyed her to avoid some punishment from the universe, he did it because weird or not, she was his mother.

Today, it meant something different. Mother had stopped him from going out this morning, saying she had plans. She looked different from normal. Her usually full-face looked gaunt, her eyes sunken. She reeked of the chemicals that she used to make her soaps, and there were little scratches and burns on her palms when she brought them up to cup his cheeks and press a kiss to his forehead. She had been up all night working again. It was not often that these frenzies of activity took her, but each time they did, the shop would be almost entirely restocked in one fell swoop, and their kitchen at home would be left looking like a train had run through it — another one of the small oddities of character that Giuseppe had never really considered too seriously before.

The things that he'd taken for granted all his life were now standing in stark contrast to the future that he'd laid out before him. For the first time, he would live a life of his own, outside of his mother's long shadow. He would have men, brothers-at-arms, all around him, and together, they'd drive back the moral degeneracy that flooded into Italy from all sides. They wouldn't quiver at the footsteps of some old woman, no matter what fortune she told for them. They'd drive back the enemies of fascism and see the world put right, with the strength of arms and the force of their will. These were solid things. Real things that nobody could deny. Not like the half-baked dreaming of his mother that, even now, in his final days trapped under her control, he marched in step with.

He was a grown man. He shouldn't be so subservient to any woman, least of all his mother. Yet, when she came to him with a tremor in her voice and a kiss on his brow, he would've done anything for her. If she'd asked him to turn aside from his course, suffer the indignity of being marked a coward, and stay home, here with her, then he would have. Pride or not, he loved his mother without condition. But all that she wanted was his help around the house. She was too short to reach the tin bath on top of the wardrobe, and she wanted him to have one last wash before he tried on his new uniform. That was the trouble with Mama's odd behaviour. It always started out sounding so calm and reasonable that it was only when the sun had set, and you were still wandering the woods looking for a very specific kind of spider's web, that you realised you'd been dragged over the precipice of madness again.

How could anyone argue with their mother suggesting they take a bath and look their best for their first time out on parade? It was the most reasonable thing that Giuseppe had ever heard coming out of her mouth, yet just one glance at her glazed expression spoke volumes. There was some great working rattling around behind her stare, some new crazed intention behind her very reasonable request. Yet still, he obeyed.

With a grunt and a heave, he fetched the corroded old bath down, and with far less complaining, he set about carrying the pans of hot water through from the wild mess of the kitchen to the silent living room where it had been set in front of the empty hearth. He might have complained about the state of the kitchen, but he couldn't deny that the soaps that she'd been making smelled absolutely delightful. It was some new recipe, rich with the usual perfumed oils, but tempered with some soft creaminess that he didn't recognise. The same intuition that led Mama down strange paths also brought her to exotic ideas. Without her adventurous spirit, he had no doubt that the soap business would have closed down years ago. She conjured new ideas as if out of thin air, and for every one that had turned his hair green or left his eyes watering at its scent, there'd been a dozen that were so good that the shop had sold out of them in weeks, with people travelling in from across the countryside around Reggio Emilia, as news spread.

He would ask her to give him a bar to take away with him when he travelled so that he could remember home each time he stopped to wash. That was the kind of sentiment that she appreciated. It might make her well up with tears, but he supposed that's what she expected of him. She would cry, but she'd be satisfied that he was going to miss her instead of suspecting that he couldn't wait to be free of her. The truth wouldn't have brought tears — it would've brought the hook-clawed, slack-mouthed rage that he'd only had the misfortune of witnessing a few times in his life. He'd rather she cried and thought kindly of him.

By the time the last pot of water had been carried through, the water had begun to cool enough that it only reddened his skin instead of blistering it. By the time that he undressed, he would be able to tolerate it. He started on the buttons of his nightshirt, but Mama wandered into the room, and he paused. She had the new soap clutched in her hands, creamy white against her raw fingers. Her stare wasn't fixed on him. It was as if he wasn't even in the room. She was lost in the labyrinth of her thoughts, chasing whatever her latest obsession was through all the twists and turns that would've left a normal woman howling in an asylum. There was no etiquette for situations like this, so Giuseppe stood paralyzed by confusion until she dragged her stare back into focus and came over to him, tutting. Those same wizened hands reached out to unbutton his shirt as he mumbled his protests, and when she abruptly yanked the cloth over his head and out of his fumbling hands, he immediately moved to cover himself, cupping his hands over his manhood.

For the first time, Mama seemed to be herself again, aware of what was happening around her. She cackled, 'You think I've never seen one before? You think I've never seen that one before? I dressed and bathed you for all your years, and now you're getting shy?'

He may have been a grown man now, but he hadn't been a grown man for long enough to refute anything she'd said to him. He bleated, 'Mama!' and tried to back away, but she had a dry hand in the small of his back now, pushing him forward towards the tub. 'In you get. Before it gets cold, come on now. Such fussing.'

When she said it, it all sounded reasonable, yet every part of him wanted to scream. This was too strange by far. He didn't like it. He stepped into the tub, if only to get away from her. He sank into the water with a soft hiss of pain, to hide as much of his bare skin from her gaze as he could.

She still wouldn't leave. She hovered there by the side of the bath, the soap snatched up from the stool and in her hand again. He reached out for it, hoping that if she could just fulfil her purpose here, she'd leave, but instead of passing it over, she took hold of his hand. 'You are very precious to me, Giuseppe.'

'I know, Mama. You're precious to me, too.' He tried to pull his hand back but succeeded in dragging her to her knees by the side of the tub. Her grip was like a vice.

'If something were to happen to you, I wouldn't be able to bear it. My heart, it would break.' She dipped the soap into the water and started rubbing it up his arm.

'Mama, I can wash myself.'

'You're my baby, and I'll always take care of you. No matter what happens. No matter what it costs. I will take care of you, Giuseppe. I promise this to you.'

He'd stopped straining now, worried that he'd drag the old woman into the tub with him. His expression softened. She was just sad that he was leaving. This was just her bizarre way of showing it, like the talismans and the chants. He smiled up at her. 'I know, Mama, I know.'

'Such a good boy.'

Mama worked the soap into a lather on his chest, and he let her. He only had to endure this discomfort for a little while, after all. He'd then, finally, be free.

Born of Hate

In 1894, Leonarda Cianciulli was born in Montella, Avellino, in the south of Italy. While the vast majority of the children in this world are born out of an act of love, Leonarda was conceived in hatred and brutality.

Emilia di Nolfi had been one of the great beauties of the small but ancient town of Montella. She was just approaching marriageable age and displaying all of the charms that could turn the head of even married men. With her looks, her good reputation, and a decent dowry on offer from her parents, she had a promising future ahead of her, with a choice of suitors and the implicit guarantee that she'd live a long, comfortable life, raising future generations of beautiful children and ruling over a grand family as their matriarch.

By contrast, Mariano Cianciulli had very little going for him. His family was destitute, his prospects extremely limited by his advancing age, cruel nature, and lack of stature within the community. It seems likely that the two of them would never have even crossed paths as they navigated the complex dance of their respective courtships, were it not for some particularly bad luck on Emilia's part.

There was no overlap between their social circles, but Montella was not so bustling a metropolis that any girl could entirely avoid being picked out in a crowd. Mariano had seen Emilia about town, and he soon developed an obsession with the pretty young woman. He saw her, and he followed her. The difference in their positions was abundantly clear to him, and he loathed her for the good luck that had placed her out of his reach. He wanted to tear her down from her pedestal, to make her no better than him. He wanted to ruin her.

One night, he got his chance. Emilia had spent another pleasant evening at a well-chaperoned dinner party with one of her suitors. Mariano had spent his time drinking a bottle of cheap wine alone in the shadows outside their estate. It was a beautiful summer night, and home wasn't far, so Emilia set off from their gates with a wave. It would be the last time in her life that she'd know happiness.

She barely made a sound when Mariano dragged her off the road into a field. To begin with, she believed it was a friend playing a prank, but as he started wrestling with her skirts, she realised that she was being robbed, and tried to protect her dignity while explaining she didn't have her purse. It wasn't her money that Mariano wanted, but she was too innocent to know that.

She'd heard some talk of what happened on a wedding night, but her family had conspired to keep any further details from her. She didn't know what he was doing when he forced up her skirts and pulled at her underclothes. She didn't know what he was doing as he climbed on top of her and forced her legs apart. Even when he penetrated her, she didn't understand what was happening. She wept and screamed at the pain until he covered her mouth, but she didn't comprehend the extent of her desecration. Not until later.

It was many hours later that she found the strength to pick herself up from the crushed crops to take herself home. She ached with every step, from the strains in her twisted limbs to the wet, burning sensation between her thighs. All that she knew was confusion and pain.

When she awoke in her bed the next morning, she assumed that it'd all been a nightmare, until she found her thighs crusted with blood and her dress all muddied. She still didn't know exactly what had happened, but Catholic shame had already kicked in. What had happened the night before was something to do with sex, and sex made you dirty, wicked, and corrupt, in the eyes of the Lord. She couldn't bear for anyone to know about her experience, so she set about cleaning herself and her dress up as quickly as possible before her parents found out and questioned her.

She thought that she'd succeeded in her deceptions. For long months, she tried to get on with her life, acting as though nothing had happened, as though everything hadn't been tainted and ruined, but it wasn't so. No matter how she tried to laugh and dance, the memory wouldn't leave her. It was like a thorn stuck in the back of her mind, always nagging at her but too painful to tug free.

Throughout all of this, Mariano watched her still, waiting to see if she'd have the guts to report him to the police, or if his plan to take her down a peg had done just that. There was no way that she could go on with her life, pretending that he didn't exist. Every time their paths crossed, he saw her eyes widen in terror, he saw the colour drain from her cheeks — She'd never forget him; not now.

The change in her temperament may have gone unnoticed by her joyfully oblivious family, but there were other, less subtle signs of what had happened to her that night. The bump itself took quite a while to show — she was young, and it was her first pregnancy — but there were other indications that her mother recognised all too readily. Eventually, she was confronted by her mother and father in private, and they demanded an explanation. When none was forthcoming, they threatened to go from house to house, visiting all of her suitors until they found the one who'd defiled her and ruined her chances of a good match. Faced with her private shame being spread all the way across town, Emilia told them the bare minimum of details. She gave the name of her rapist. She told them the night it had happened. And she said nothing more.

Imagine her horror when Mariano and the other Cianciulli family members were arrayed around her dining room table the next night, and conversation had turned to how the boy was going to make things right. There was only one way that things could be settled as far as Emilia's parents were concerned. The only way to maintain their daughter's honour was for Mariano to marry her immediately.

They didn't have to ask him twice. This was everything that he'd dreamed of since he first laid eyes on her — the beautiful, perfect di Nolfi daughter on his arm and in his marital bed. It was more than he could've ever dreamed of. With his assent, a date was rapidly set for the wedding, and a discrete priest was brought into the conversation to make things official.

Whatever grand dreams Emilia had of a white dress and a party with all of her friends were dragged through the gutters by the hushed and hurried ceremony. Then, when it was over, she and her new husband had to carry her bags down to their new home together. They hadn't spoken to each other since he raped her. They hadn't said a single word to one another through the wedding planning and their parents' negotiations. Once Mariano had given his assent to marrying her, their part in the decision making was done.

They didn't have one of the grand houses that Emilia had been accustomed to. They didn't even have the kind of unpainted townhouse that Mariano had been accustomed to. Their new home was a hovel in the poorest part of town. It had no furniture to speak of, and the bathroom was outside and shared with the others on the row of houses. Mariano had no job, and his prospects weren't getting better with a pregnant wife in tow.

The first few days were traumatic for Emilia. Everything that she'd ever known had just been stripped away from her, and all that she had for comfort was the man who'd ruined her life. When her lack of enthusiasm became obvious on their very first night together, Mariano forced himself on her again and again. He slapped her around when she didn't keep the house tidy enough for his liking, despite her having domestic servants to handle such things since she was a baby. She had no idea about any of the wifely duties that Mariano had assigned to her, and he took her lack of understanding to be rebellion, which he was intent on stomping out. Understandably, she was terrified of him, but the people around her that might've been able to offer solace had none to spare.

In the eyes of the poor of Montella, Emilia was getting exactly what she deserved. If she hadn't wanted to be dragged down from her ivory tower to live life like the rest of the normal people, then she shouldn't have succumbed to her carnal desires. Worse yet, all of high society had entirely turned its back on her. Even her mother, whom she had expected to defend her to the last, had listened to her tales of woe and treated her with the same contempt as the poor black-eyed wives that she now went to market alongside. If she didn't want to marry Mariano and live the life that he could bring her, then she shouldn't have given up her purity to him.

And so her degradation and torment went on and on, until one muggy April night, the worst pain that she'd ever experience racked her. Since the beginning of the year, her stomach had continued to bloat, as often with hunger as with pregnancy, but in the last few weeks before the coming of the blood and screaming, she had grown to almost comical proportions. She clung to her swollen stomach through the long miserable nights of spring and shielded it from Mariano's fists when he turned them on her.

It seemed that it hadn't been enough because now she was in agony. Mariano had wandered off to go drinking with his buddies, and her neighbours had proven, time and again, that they wouldn't come calling if they heard screaming. She was entirely alone in the world with the molten lead agony of a baby demanding release.

After what felt like days, she managed to make her way out into the streets. She grappled with the passing drunks begging for help until, finally, one of the local women took pity on her and sent a runner to the town's midwife. The labour was long and arduous, with Emilia slipping in and out of consciousness throughout the process, but finally, among blood and agony, Leonarda Cianciulli was born.

It would've been nice if she'd been the one bright light at the end of Emilia's miserable journey, but for the first few days, her mother was so exhausted that she went barely noticed. When the baby had been inside her, it had all felt like a dream, like there was still some way for it to go away and for her life to return to normal. But now, she had the mewling little thing latched onto her chest like a leech, demanding attention every moment of the day, denying her even the brief respite of sleep. It would've been nice if she could look down at her baby and feel some pride in the life she'd brought into the world, some joy. But all that Emilia could see was her downfall and the pain that Mariano had caused her.

In the years that followed, Emilia, Mariano, and Leonarda moved about town several times as they were thrown out of home after home due to their destitution. It didn't even seem to register with Mariano — he was too intent on pursuing his hedonistic pleasures to ever concern himself with the little details of paying the rent or working for a living. Emilia and Leonarda survived, for the most part, thanks to the kindness of others, mostly funnelled to them through the church. The donations that they received were a source of constant shame for Emilia, yet without them, she and her daughter would almost certainly have died.

For her part, Leonarda remembered little of those early days, with only a vague recollection of doom and guilt hanging over her. She couldn't recall her father at all in later life, only her mother, and those weren't happy memories.

Emilia felt powerless. The only control that she had over her life had been stripped away when she was raped — not even her own body was her own. Her husband could take her and do what he pleased with her at a moment's notice. She'd gone from having the world in the palm of her hand to having less than nothing. The only thing in the world that she could exert any sort of power over was Leonarda, so that is exactly what she did. All of her frustration and misery were poured down into her daughter. The toddler was beaten for the slightest infraction. Every waking moment was a litany of barbed criticism. Everything that Emilia would never dare to say to her husband, she spat with venom at the girl-child who'd become the symbol of her downfall. By day, she poured hatred and loathing into her daughter, and by night, she suffered fresh torments and indignities if and when Mariano staggered home drunk. In her brief moments of silent contemplation, she prayed for release from this hell that she'd been condemned to through no fault of her own, and one day, three years into her marriage, those prayers were answered. Mariano stopped coming home.

It would take several days before Emilia even realised that something was amiss. Mariano's drinking binges would sometimes stretch out over days at a time, so this absence was barely worthy of note. It was only then that she went out wandering the streets with her daughter in tow, looking for the husband that she hated so much out of some sense of propriety. Eventually, she found him camped out in the home of one of his friends. He'd been running a fever and fallen into a deep sleep that nobody could wake him from.

Nobody had the money for a doctor, and even if they had, they wouldn't have wasted it on a man like Mariano. With some help from Mariano's fellow alcoholics, they transported him back to the latest hovel where the Cianciulli family had been staying and abandoned him to his wife's tender care.

Emilia didn't even go through the motions of trying to nurse him back to health. While he lay there in their marital bed, lost in a coma and creeping ever closer to death, Emilia slept soundly on the cot with Leonarda, shoving the girl out of her one place of comfort in the world. For the first time in years, Emilia allowed herself to dream. Soon she would be a widow, and, with that, there'd be freedom. She would have to mourn publicly for a time, but then she could begin courting again. She may have lost some of the ripeness of youth by this point, but she could still turn some heads once she was cleaned up. This was a chance for a new beginning, a new husband, and a new life.

The day of the funeral stretched long and dull for young Leonarda. She understood little of the hustle of activity and ceremony around her. She'd been told that her father was dead, but it meant little to her. She'd seen him slightly less often and cared for him as little as she always had. What wore on her wasn't grief; it was the boredom. Her mother kept Leonarda waiting by the side of the grave while all the well-wishers came by and placed a kiss on her cheek. Both sides of the family were united one last time to offer up their condolences, and it was all that Emilia could do to keep the smile from her lips. She waited them all out until even the gravediggers were done filling in the hole and had headed home for their dinner. It was only then that she finally stepped forward, bent at the waist, and spat onto Mariano's grave. 'That man was a pig, and it's for the best that we're rid of him.'

Once again, things didn't go quite according to Emilia's plans, however. She'd thought that, in the aftermath of her husband's death, her family would welcome her back to their estate with open arms, but in their eyes, she was an independent agent now — not a part of their family anymore but an interloper who'd married out. Whatever financial or emotional support she thought would come flooding back in now that Mariano was gone, wasn't forthcoming. She'd become a cautionary tale for the other young women of Montella — don't sleep with men, or else look what will happen to you. The di Nolfi family didn't want to invite that shame back under their roof, so she was ignored, side-lined, and forgotten.

With no help forthcoming, she cut her mourning period short and began courting again in short order, abandoning Leonarda to take care of herself in the evenings, while she went out dancing and drinking. The balls and extravagant meals of high society eluded her, but the middle class of Montella didn't object strongly to her joining their ranks. Sadly, the interest of most men in the widow Cianciulli was more carnal than romantic. The men pursuing her did so because they thought that she was an opportunity to sow their wild oats before settling into arranged marriages; that or they had some defect that prevented them from landing a wife without her sordid history. The criminals and scum of Montella flocked around her, and before long, she found herself considering them. They were the only ones that seemed to offer her any opportunity to advance herself, and if society was going to reject her anyway, then why shouldn't she break its rules?

Her second husband was more financially solvent than Mariano had been, but not by much. He'd impressed Emilia through their courtship with his extravagant spending, but that same extravagant spending soon burned through all of the money that he brought into the household. He lavished gifts of perfume and fine clothes on his wife, but their home was still little better than the hovels she'd become accustomed to. Money came to him easily, but it slipped right through his fingers. If anything, this lifestyle was even more chaotic for young Leonarda than the steady misery of her father's care. She was frequently left alone as Emilia went out with her husband to eat his earnings, surviving on leftovers and scraps. Her fortunes were changed very little by the addition of a new father. Nobody seemed to care for Leonarda any more than they had before. Her mother's emotional and physical abuse were maintained at the same crushing level, and her step-father cared nothing for her, only for the beautiful wife he'd managed to procure for himself. If anything, the abuse became worse now that Emilia was happier. Every time that she looked at her daughter, she was reminded of the worst time in her life, and she lashed out as a result.

Alone in the world, riddled with anxiety and self-loathing, it didn't take long before the barely formed psyche of young Leonarda began to crumble under the weight of her mother's loathing. She wasn't even a teenager the first time that she attempted suicide. She made a noose for herself by tying together the filthy bedsheets and slinging them over the exposed rafters of the portioned-up farmhouse where they'd been staying. Her knot-tying wasn't up to the task, with her makeshift noose coming apart before it could kill her, but even so, she spent a week unable to speak after crushing her larynx in the attempt. If her mother even noticed, she made no comment.

Her second suicide attempt came less than a year later, when she was 13, and followed much the same pattern, but once again, fate seemed to intervene to save the girl from death.

The only prospect of escape from the hell that her mother seemed so intent on keeping her in was marriage. As she moved on through her teenage years, Leonarda would develop the looks that had drawn so many men to Emilia, and prospects to match. Emilia was all too aware of the possibilities of a good match for Leonarda. The sins of the mother hadn't been passed down to the child, as far as the Montello community was concerned, so there was no reason that the girl's beauty couldn't be parleyed into the kind of high society marriage that Emilia herself had always dreamed of. Leonarda was a chance to set right what had gone wrong with her life and to create a steady pension for herself and her new husband by tapping her daughter's new husband for financial support.

While none of the old connections in society had served Emilia in the past, she now found that doors were opened to her once more, now that she had something worth buying. A pristine, beautiful young woman from the di Nolfi line, with none of the preconceived attachments that a normal girl in high society would carry along with her. Leonarda represented quite a catch for a certain kind of man. For her part, Emilia enjoyed a return to the luxurious lifestyle of her youth when she went visiting on courtship business. She dawdled about it instead of making a swift decision, because she was enjoying this brief window of being treated with respect again so much. That delay proved to be her undoing.

Unknown to Emilia, Leonarda had been making enquiries with regards to a husband and, lacking in high society connections or knowledge of etiquette, she'd been engaging in what the modern world would probably consider dating, but what in 1917 was considered scandalous. Marriage was the only escape available to Leonarda, and since her mother hadn't deigned to inform her of the plans that she was making regarding her daughter's future, Leonarda had to take matters into her own hands.

By the time that Leonarda had turned twenty-three, she was more than ready to be out from under her mother's shadow and into the world. Yet, still, Emilia dawdled, taking tea with this lady to discuss her son's proposition, then lunch with some widower about his nephew's interests. The list of Emilia's choices of potential suitors grew with each passing day, while by the end of 1917, Leonarda had narrowed her options down to just a single man, which was when all hell broke loose.

The Cursed Marriage

There would be no grand ceremony for Leonarda, not any more than there'd been for her mother. Yet, she marched to her fate with a bounce in her step. The man that she'd chosen for herself, Raffaele Pansardi, was several years her senior, barely established in a low paying government clerk job that nonetheless would provide the couple with stability throughout all their years together. It wasn't the kind of grandeur that her mother's planned matches would've created, but it would provide her with a life with no ups and downs. The nervous disposition that Leonarda had developed in response to her mother's decades of abuse demanded that kind of stability, above all else.

Of course, Emilia didn't see it that way. When Leonarda approached her mother with Raffaele's proposal, Emilia dismissed it out of hand. The stupid girl clearly had no idea what she was doing, and she should wait for her mother to partner her up with someone more befitting her lineage. Yet again, the contempt with which she treated her daughter would be her undoing. If she'd merely informed Leonarda of her plans for her, then it was likely that the girl would've gone along with them. Instead, it appeared to Leonarda that her mother was denying her the only possibility of escape from their hellish life together, out of pure spite.

Leonarda had never gone against her mother's wishes, never even argued with her — Mother always knew best. That was the only way she could survive the onslaught of insults and berating that followed even the slightest sign of rebellion. Yet now, for the first time, she girded herself against the impending assault and moved forward with her plans. Perhaps she consoled herself with the thought that she'd be escaping her mother's reach, or perhaps she'd just reached her breaking point. Regardless, she accepted Raffaele's proposal, and the two were soon wed in a small ceremony with his family and her friends from around town. Her mother didn't attend.

When she returned to the hovel she'd called home all of her life to collect her few sparse belongings, Emilia ambushed her, not with a physical attack, but with the coldest words that she'd ever doled out to her loathed daughter. She cursed Leonarda's marriage. There was no great speech about how she'd betrayed her mother's trust, no reveal of the amazing life that she'd missed out on by defying her wishes, only the simple curse, spat at Leonarda with all the certainty that Emilia possessed.

Nothing could've been more devastating to Leonarda. She'd readied herself for abuse, but this felt like the ultimate dismissal. Her mother's fury was such that she didn't even have words to express it anymore. All that she had was hatred, expressed as purely as it could be with the desire for nothing but evil things to happen to Leonarda.

That curse followed Leonarda for the rest of her life. At this point, chaos had reigned over her existence for so long that the very idea of any underlying order was appealing, even when the mystical underpinnings of her worldview meant that suffering was on the cards. She'd always believed in the supernatural, as was normal for young women of the time, but now she was faced with the reality of that belief. She truly believed that her mother's words had power, and they haunted her.

She did her best to avoid her mother from that point forward, but she needn't have bothered. Even when their paths did cross, Emilia acted as though she didn't see the girl. It was as if the older woman's dearest wish had finally come true — she was living her life as though her daughter didn't exist. The first few years of the marriage, what should've been the happiest time in Leonarda's life, was marred by misfortune.

Her nervous disposition was no longer reinforced by her mother's berating, but instead, an internal critic had taken up the mantle of abuser. Nobody needed to tell Leonarda she was failing in her role as a wife when she was so convinced of it herself. Raffaele was a kind and reasonable man who couldn't understand his wife's eccentricities. He didn't understand why she wept when his dinner was burnt or cowered away from him when she stained the washing. He couldn't understand why every minor inconvenience seemed to be a huge dramatic crisis in her mind.

With time, it's likely that Leonarda might've found her way back to sanity and calm, but it was in these first few years of her marriage that her health began to fail her. She was taken by fits and seizures when she became too emotional, and given that she was a bundle of nerves even at the best of times, this exacerbated her condition terribly. It seems likely that she suffered from epilepsy, but an official diagnosis was never made. She felt no need to go to the doctor for an explanation when her sickness was clearly the result of her mother's curse finally taking effect. Soon, the seizures became a self-fulfilling prophecy. Leonarda would become emotional because she was afraid of having an attack, which led to her having an attack. Every time that the creeping sense of doom that characterised her experience of the world became too intense, she suffered a painful fit, just proving her worldview to be correct.

Raffaele did what he could to support his wife, but things weren't going well for him, either. It wasn't only her mother that Leonarda had crossed when she made her marriage arrangements. Many of his superiors in the local government had intimate ties to the local nobility, and that whole subsection of society disapproved of his match to Leonarda. When it came time for advancement at work, Raffaele found himself overlooked again and again. Even the small benefits that his co-workers enjoyed seemed to pass him by. It became apparent to him that life in Montello was never going to be smooth sailing, but he truly loved Leonarda, and he wasn't going to let something as insignificant as the contempt of all society stand between them.

Leonarda had always feared the travelling Romani thanks to her mother's horror stories about them — even though she'd inherited Romani blood on her father's side — but now desperation drove her to seek them out. She found a fortune teller at a seasonal fayre and begged her for a reading. With reluctance, the palm reader led her into her stall and sat her down. Before the reading could even begin, Leonarda yelped out, 'Am I going to die? Is that what the curse is going to do?' Frowning, the fortune teller took hold of her hands and drew them closer, tracing Leonarda's life-line with a fingertip. 'No. You're not going to die. Not for a long time.'

Relief flooded through Leonarda. She would've toppled from her seat if the fortune teller wasn't still holding onto her hands. The headaches and seizures weren't a sign that the curse was killing her; they were just some sickness. She didn't need to be afraid. She was so relieved that she almost missed the next thing that the fortune teller said. 'You're going to live a long life, full of sadness. You will outlive every one of your children.'

Leonarda snatched her hands back, but it was already too late. She'd already heard the terrible future that lay ahead of her. She threw her coin at the fortune teller and ran for home, tears streaming down her face. She couldn't think of any worse punishment that her mother could've inflicted on her than this. She couldn't think of any greater cruelty that any woman could've done to another than to take the gift that she had for creating life and turning it against her.

The truest proof of the curse came to Leonarda three years into her marriage. Despite the economic instability that plagued them and her constantly fluctuating health, the couple still had every intention of living a normal wedded life, and that included children. She'd expected to have no trouble in that regard — her mother had told her often of the cursed fertility that had created her marriage to Mariano. Leonarda had every expectation that, as soon as they started trying for children, she'd be surrounded by a brood of them, yet that didn't seem to be the case.

It took three years before she first became pregnant. With the tiny life nestled within her, Leonarda's anxiety was driven into overdrive. She had to protect her baby from the curse. She had to do everything that she could to keep it safe. In turn, the spike in anxiety brought on more epileptic seizures, and with those seizures, falls.

Within three months of learning that she was pregnant, Leonarda suffered her first miscarriage. She wasn't as uneducated on the subject of sex and reproduction as her mother — times had changed considerably over the past few decades — but even so, she had no idea what was happening to her until the midwife arrived to check on her. She lay in her bed for hours, frantic with terror, racked by fits each time that her anxiety reached a fever pitch, and soaked in blood. In such circumstances, it's hardly surprising that she believed she was cursed.

This latest horror to be inflicted on the fledgling family was the straw the broke the camel's back. As long as they lived in her mother's shadow, Leonarda believed that the curse would doom them. Given his situation at work, Raffaele was inclined to agree that leaving was the best option. In 1920, the pair of them packed up their meagre belongings and took the train out of town, never to return. Nobody came to see them off. Literal or not, the curse hung over them, and it didn't encourage the people of Montella to associate with the Pansardis.

Over the next year, the couple moved several times, each time getting further and further from Montella. They took on temporary jobs to make ends meet, scrabbling with the other itinerant workers that travelled Italy in search of work, and struggling to keep food in their bellies and a roof over their heads. This made Leonarda's anxiety worse and led to more seizures, which, in turn, ruined her chances at steady employment.

Finally, in 1921, the couple settled more permanently in Raffaele's childhood home of Lauria, Potenza. They'd gathered enough money in their last agricultural job to lay down a deposit on a small house, and soon, with the two of them working, they were able to finally build some sort of life for themselves. They'd travelled over a hundred miles from their old home before they dared to put down roots, but the warmer climate of southern Italy seemed to agree with the two of them. So far from her mother's influence, Leonarda's anxiety seemed to abate, and with a roof over their heads and steady paycheques flowing, she began to feel some of the safety and stability that she'd always longed for. In Lauria, with Raffaele's family there to support them, they decided to start trying for a family again.

With some time and distance, Leonarda had begun to believe that the curse her mother had put upon them wasn't real. Raffaele had always described her problems as being related to a nervous temperament rather than ascribing any supernatural cause to her troubles, and she'd begun to adopt the same way of thinking. She even began to believe it. If she could just make herself calm, then perhaps the children that she longed for would be born, instead of rotting on the vine.

In 1922, Leonarda gave birth to her eldest son, Giuseppe. It was as if all of the suffering and hardship of the lifetime before was washed away the moment that Leonarda held him. He was perfect in every way, the child she'd longed for ever since she married Raffaele. It was clear to her then that their fortunes were changing, that they'd escaped her mother's curse. Finally, they would be free to live their own lives beyond her influence. Finally, fate would leave them to their own devices.

The pregnancy had been painless compared to her previous nightmarish attempts at carrying a child to term, and she took to motherhood with a single-minded devotion that put even her obsession with marriage to shame. Every waking moment was devoted to Giuseppe, to caring for him, pampering him and preparing a future for him that was much brighter than the one that she'd endured.

Money was the trouble. Security had always been her goal in life. It had driven her to choose her partner, and now it drove her to seek out more and more wealth with which to establish a safety net for her son. If she could raise enough money that minor inconveniences like a change of job or a rise in rent were no longer existential threats, then she felt certain that peace, health, and happiness would soon follow after.

She applied for every job in town, seeking out the same kind of clerical work that her husband had secured for himself, but nobody wanted to hire her. She was condemned to 'women's work' like tending a bar and wiping tables in the local taverns. It made her a pittance, and the constant noise amped up her anxiety to ridiculous levels. With no better options, she persevered, even as it caused her seizures to flare up again.

With Leonarda so obviously well-suited to motherhood, and with the support network of Raffaele's extended family in place to help them out, it seemed only natural that the couple would try again for more of the same blessings. What followed was a gruesome reminder that misfortune would follow them wherever they went. Another miscarriage. Brought on by falls and seizures, or just her body rejecting the life that was growing inside her.

Giuseppe became even more of a miracle in her eyes with each failed pregnancy. The one child who'd survived the curse — surely, the most important child in the world to have overcome such odds.

Despite that latest horror, Leonarda and Raffaele tried for children again and again through the years, and finally, it seemed that their luck had changed. Leonarda gave birth to two girls in quick succession, then another boy soon after. The family that she'd been craving through all of the sad and bloody years was finally coming together before her eyes. For Leonarda, the joy that she felt as she held each child in her arms was only slightly greater than the relief of bringing the babies to term, that she was beating the curse at last.

They then began to sicken. It was just a minor illness here and there, at first, not enough for Leonarda to see a pattern beginning to form. One of the girls had bad lungs and coughed her way through the nights. The boy was covered in rashes every few days. Then, these minor ailments grew more serious. The coughing was incessant, filling any moment of peace in the house. The little girl's lungs were thick with fluid, drowning her each time she lay down. Leonarda spent sleepless nights with the girl propped up against her chest, just so her daughter could get some sleep, but in the end, even that wasn't enough. The toddler died in her mother's arms.

The baby boy was soon to follow his sister to the grave. Before Leonarda had even finished grieving for one of her children, the next was found cold and dead in his cot. There was no explanation that the doctors could offer beyond bad luck, and nobody had the heart to hack the baby apart to find out if it had been born with some deformity that had ended its life so prematurely.

Leonarda's grieving was a terrible thing to see. She tore chunks of her hair from her scalp, abandoned her part-time jobs entirely, and devoted every waking moment to paranoid observation of her surviving children.

As the years rolled by, her paranoia grew worse. She wouldn't let Giuseppe out to play on his own, not without her watching him at all times, and with so many younger children in the home, he was as trapped there as his mother.

Each time that her grief abated enough, Raffaele would convince her to start over again, and there'd be another nine months of terror, just waiting for the miscarriages to start all over again. There were no miscarriages, but each of Leonarda's children sickened and died before they reached their third year. Five little boys died, and Leonarda's sanity crumbled a little more with each child that she was forced to bury.

Raffaele had always been gentle with his wife, always aware that his earnings were less than she really needed and that she'd chosen him over far more worthwhile suitors out of love. Yet, even he could recognise that her attachment to the children was becoming unhealthy. Even the boy and girl that had survived their early years were in danger of being smothered with her constant attention. He was smart enough not to make any attempt to pry the children from her hands, phrasing his request in a way that made the failure of judgement seem like it was his rather than hers. They needed more money with their ever-growing family, and he wasn't able to advance any further in his job for the foreseeable future. Leonarda was going to have to work, but she rebelled at the idea. How could she leave her precious children unattended when doom might fall on them at any moment? The whole universe was conspiring to snatch her children from her grasp. Abandoning them to that fate without even their mother there to care for them was madness.

The longer she spent in the children's constant company, the more unhinged she became. Every little whimper that a child made was cause for alarm. Every child that slept soundly was stirred by Leonarda's shaking to make sure that they were still breathing. There would be no peace for the family unless Leonarda could rediscover her equilibrium.

Raffaele asked around town for work that might suit his wife, and while she was too unstable to secure any of the customer service jobs that she'd held in their earlier marriage, there were plenty of places where she could work that were out of the public eye. He managed to secure a job for her as the cleaner for the town's bank and pressured her into attending with talk about the children going hungry. Raffaele was well-known as a reliable and trustworthy man, and there was an assumption that she'd follow in his footsteps, taking good care of the building in the evenings after all of the clerks had departed. The peace of working alone in the evenings was ideal for Leonarda, as was the work itself. There was something deeply satisfying about taking a place that was dirty and making it clean. Though the bank had plenty of money to throw around, very little of it was spent on cleaning supplies. Leonarda had to learn how to mix her soaps and detergents from raw materials to get the place clean, and she found some satisfaction in that simple task, too, experimenting over the nights with different mixtures until she was quite proficient.

Whatever satisfaction she drew from her working life dwindled when it came time to cash her paycheque. Her earnings were a pittance, nowhere near enough to put aside the nest egg she so desperately craved. The family could afford to eat and pay their rent, but savings remained a distant dream. The job helped her to lean back from the precipice of despair that the death of so many children had left her on, but it wasn't sufficient to drag her back towards sanity. All it would take was one last nudge, and the mask of sanity that she'd so carefully constructed for herself would crumble.

It was while she was off at work and the children were in Raffaele's care that their tenth child died. Nobody rushed to tell her — nobody wanted to be the one to share such awful news. She didn't find out that they would be burying another baby until she came home exhausted from another long night of work.

Even doing all that'd been asked of her wasn't enough. Even caring for the children all day and working all night hadn't been sufficient to keep doom from their door. She laid her last baby to rest in the same pauper's grave that the others had been consigned to and returned to work the next night. Whatever restraint that might've been holding her back in the past was entirely gone now. She'd toppled over the precipice of despair and landed in desperation. She needed more. She needed enough money to call out the doctor at the first sign of sickness. She needed a house outside of the city, where disease spread so readily. She needed enough money to make all of their problems a thing of the past.

In the bank, she had no access to the cash overnight, but she had ready access to the ledgers and records. She created a false account and simply noted that it contained the money she considered to be a reasonable amount to form her nest egg. To her mind, it was a matter of life and death to have that money, to save all of the children that she'd yet to lose.

The owners of the bank didn't agree. The 'clerical error' that had appeared in their books hadn't gone unnoticed, and when Leonarda, whom everyone knew was just a poor cleaner, came to clear out the account one day, the police escorted her out of the building.

For her fraud, she was convicted, sentenced, and imprisoned in 1927. In all likelihood, her husband would've had his name dragged through the dirt, too, if she hadn't made it so abundantly clear in her confession that she'd worked alone, "seized by madness."

The legal system of 1920s Italy was still in the process of solidifying after the nation's unification in the late 1800s. To the letter of the law, women were to receive exactly the same punishment as men for the same crimes, yet stipulations were made in the legal code to allow women to serve short sentences on house arrest, or for longer sentences, be confined to a 'special institution' built to house female prisoners. Before the unification of Italy, the legal systems of the various city-states were often little more than medieval dungeons deployed against any enemies of the noble family in power. As such, post-unification Italy had done all that it could to foster an air of fairness and even liberality when it came to their prisons. While the actual institutions where men were held remained the same grim and terrifying buildings of the old order, the interiors were kept clean and carefully regulated by the Minister for the Interior. Sadly, for women, the situation was entirely different. While the old dungeons had been converted quite successfully into modern prisons for men, there was no similar structure available to the state to house the minority of female prisoners. Luckily, there was one longstanding institution in Italy that was accustomed to jailing women for long periods, often for no greater crime than being young and rebellious: the Church. Almost every city had a reformatory where young women who might damage their family's honour were sent to live out their days quietly until they could be married off to a husband with a strong enough hand to control them. It was to one of these repurposed reformatories that Leonarda was sent to suffer out her sentence, a building that had once been a nunnery but now held every female prisoner from the entire province under the watchful eye of the institution's mother superior.

The nuns weren't known for kindness or fairness. Life in the prison was bleak, and additional years were added to many sentences at the whim of whichever nun was in charge at any given moment. The only option for women confined there, if they wanted to see the light of day again, was complete and utter subservience. Luckily for Leonarda, she had 20 years of experience trying to placate a distant and cruel mother figure who'd never be satisfied that she was good enough. With her childhood as training, she served only her initial 18-month sentence before being returned into her husband's care.

Throughout it all, there'd been one thought sustaining her — Giuseppe. Her son was out there in the harsh world with no mother to care for him. What would Raffaele know of preparing the boy's meals? Of singing the songs that she had to sing so that her baby could find his rest? Nobody except her could care for Giuseppe, and nobody would. Her other children had always been an afterthought compared to her most beloved son — an interruption or a cause for worry and grief — but Giuseppe had remained her whole world, and was the only child to completely escape the touch of the curse that she was now more certain than ever had followed her.

Everything that the family had been working for in Lauria had been snatched away by her one act of criminality. The people who'd welcomed them with open arms when they first travelled there were disgusted with her. Raffaele had lost his job due to the suspicion that she'd brought upon him, and even the Pansardi family now turned their back on the young family to preserve their precious family honour.

While honour demanded that the Pansardis turn their backs on Raffaele, there was still some affection for him and his children within the family. Even Leonarda wasn't treated entirely unfairly. The family had seen her nervous temperament through the years and expected something considerably more dramatic to go awry than a little bit of fraud. To help the couple along, a little money was passed down through the grapevine of distant relations and family friends so that they could make a new start somewhere far away and out of sight.

Once more, they packed their bags and set out into the wider world with nowhere to call home.

Dark Fortunes

There was no possibility of roaming the countryside, sleeping in haystacks, and finding work where they could. Not anymore — not with children in tow. To make matters worse, Leonarda found that her once pliant husband now seemed to have grown a spine, telling her what to do and where to go. It reminded her entirely too much of her mother. She understood that she'd made a foolish decision back in Lauria, but it had been for the very best reason — to provide her son with the kind of future that her husband had failed to. Just as Raffaele was now becoming more critical of his wife's eccentricities, so too was she now starting to see him in the same light that her mother had. He wasn't an impressive man. He didn't have any grand prospects. It was true that he loved her, and she, him, but in practical terms, these things amounted to very little. She had no house, no savings, none of the things that a wife might expect. The fact that her lack was due to her actions meant nothing to her because she felt that she'd been spurred on by her husband's lack of ambition. If Raffaele had done his job, then she wouldn't have had to commit fraud.

Still, this new and assertive Raffaele did seem to have his uses. He secured a decent clerical job for himself in the town of Lacedonia, Avellino, by letter, and loaded the family onto a train further south, once more. Lacedonia was a town much the same as the ones they'd lived in before, small, bordering on rural, but populous enough for them to disappear into the crowd after only a few short months in residence.

With the job came a small house overlooking the Osento River. It was some of the most coveted real estate in the town, raised enough to avoid the autumnal flooding of the river but close enough that the breeze could carry cool air up from the water to bathe their home, even in the height of summer. Giuseppe and the other children took to their new home like fish to water, and with the security of Raffaele's new job and more active control over their finances, she was able to relax into her role as a full-time housekeeper and mother.

It suited her well. She doted on Giuseppe and soon found herself pregnant once again. The calm of her new life became brittle. Leonarda was convinced that this new comfortable life would soon be spoiled by her mother's curse, and she suspected, with no small amount of evidence, that fate would turn against her with another bloody miscarriage.

For all that Lacedonia was a small town, it was also situated close to the main thoroughfare through Avellino. Travellers would stop in town quite frequently, and among those travellers were caravans of the Romani that her mother had always warned her against in her childhood. Leonarda's superstitions about curses had passed to her through stories about 'the evil eye' being cast on those who crossed the travelling folk, and the almost habitual warding 'horns' hand gesture that she used every time she spoke of her misfortunes was learned from those tales, too. She had those two fingers of her hand extended as she walked into the Romani camp. Her other hand was clamped down on Giuseppe's fingers with such ferocity that they were turning pale. She was afraid of the fortune teller that her friends in town had spoken of, but her need to know far outweighed that fear.

In the tent that the old woman had set up for this purpose, Leonarda held out her quaking hands and asked to be told her future. She expected to hear of a lifetime of sorrow, suffering under her mother's curse. She expected to hear a litany of death and misery. What the fortune-teller told her was completely different. 'In one hand, I can see prison. In the other, a mental asylum.' Leonarda was stunned into silence. Prison was no new spectre to hang over her, but an insane asylum was something else entirely — the kind of hell that nobody escaped from once they'd been confined. Women's prisons may not have been regulated, and the nuns may have had free reign to inflict whatever cruelties they wished upon their charges, but at least there was an end to imprisonment. These were the days before psychopharmacology had made any strides. Even Freud's ideas of psychoanalysis were struggling to find a foothold at this point in history. For the most part, if a person was deemed insane, it was comparable to a death sentence. There could be no cure; there could be no release, only eternal confinement in facilities that weren't fit to hold wild animals, let alone suffering people. This prediction was worse than anything Leonarda could have feared. She paid the fortune teller and hurried home, dragging Giuseppe all the way, just waiting for the next blow to fall.

When she gave birth to a healthy baby boy, Leonarda was more confused than anything else. She cared for the baby, as was her duty, but it was in a shell-shocked silence that worried her husband. She still showered all of her affections on Giuseppe as she always had, but the new baby received only workman-like attention. This child wasn't the miracle her firstborn had been; it was cause for suspicion. Why would the universe reward her with another healthy child, now?

The sense of impending doom that had been haunting Leonarda since she first fell pregnant again continued to grow, without the outlet of a miscarriage. She knew that something terrible was about to happen; she just couldn't work out when.

With her increasing anxiety, her epileptic fits returned, and she soon became afraid to pick up the baby in case she dropped it during one of her seizures. Life ground to a halt, with the family home that she'd loved becoming a prison that she couldn't leave for fear of harming the baby.

Only in the evenings when Raffaele had come home from work did she dare to roam, and every night that she was free, she found her feet carrying her out to the edge of the woodlands, where the Romani made camp when they were passing by.

Over and over, she visited the fortune-tellers and charlatans who travelled by Lacedonia. The doom hanging over her still had no outlet, no release, so she hunted for it. The fortune-tellers soon came to know her and expect her visits in the evenings, furnishing her with the details of their craft in exchange for yet more of Raffaele's hard-earned money.

Over the months, she began to acquire a library of books on the subject of fortune-telling, searching through each one in a vain attempt to find some way to circumvent her imagined fate. It would prove to be, ultimately, useless. While she learned how to read the fortunes of others from her time with the Romani and her books, there was no way for her to predict what was going to happen next.

When harvest time came to Lacedonia, the working people of the farms abandoned their homes to go sleep in the fields. The worst of the summer's heat was beginning to abate, and the warm nights were perfect for camping out under the stars. Almost all work in town ground to a halt during the harvest as workers abandoned their usual tasks to join the people in the field. Leonarda's friends all headed out into the fields to join in with the work, so she and the children followed along afterwards, caught up in the festival atmosphere. Even Raffaele found himself alone when he arrived at his offices, abandoning his desk for the durum wheat fields before the sun had reached its zenith. The whole town worked together throughout the day, and for the first time, as she moved beneath the blazing sun, Leonarda forgot all about the doom that had been plaguing her since she conceived her second son. Out here, among the smiling, real people of the town, it seemed obvious that all this talk of fate and curses was just a figment of her overactive imagination.

As night fell, people gathered around to feast together in the fields. There was music and dancing. With no doom hanging over her, Leonarda had no fear of rising to her feet and joining her husband as they frolicked around the fire. Thoughts of suffering and seizures fled from her mind as Raffaele embraced her, and at the end of the night, when her feet were tired from dancing, the four of them, their little family, nestled around each other on a mattress of cut wheat and slept with sweet dreams.

It was still dark when Leonarda was shaken awake. She reached out to stop whoever was doing it, but her hands found only air. Her eyes snapped open, and she sprang upright. Around her, in the field, she could hear groaning as others stirred from their sleep. Whatever spirit had just seized her had disturbed all of them, as well. The wheat in the fields was shivering, as though some great wind was sweeping across the planes, but none of them could feel a breeze. Some of the women began to murmur amongst themselves about omens and ghosts. Still, the minutes ticked by with nothing more happening, so, gradually, they all began to relax. Perhaps it had just been an unexpected wind stirring the unsettled from their sleep. Perhaps there'd been some sound, a baby crying out, or an animal's call up on the hills that had stirred them from their rest. They returned to their places on the ground and tried to drift off to sleep once more, but doom-haunted Leonarda couldn't. She knew what she'd felt. She knew that the eye of fate was upon her and that some dark spirit had just washed over the town of Lacedonia. Yet, even she couldn't manufacture any more evidence to support her anxiety, so she sank to the wheat beside her husband and clung to him for whatever comfort he could give her.

An hour trickled by, and everyone who'd been disturbed sank back into the embrace of sleep. All except Leonarda. She lay in the darkness, staring up at the baleful stars that outlined the fate of everyone gathered here beneath them. She shivered, despite the heat. Something bad was coming. She could feel it in her bones.

The next tremor woke anyone who was still sleeping. The baby at Leonarda's side began to cry, a piercing shriek in the darkness. She scooped it up but didn't dare to stand for fear that one of her seizures would wrack her and make her drop her son. The terror in her bones had already spread to her muscles — every inch of her was shuddering. She rolled over to lay the screaming baby in Raffaele's arms before the fit could take her, but she then realised that he was shaking, too. This wasn't one of her fits. The whole world was shaking. More screams started up in the fields around her, women and children shaken from their rest, confronted with a world of chaos that they could never have predicted, which lay just beneath the surface of their perfectly ordered lives. For the first time, they all saw the world as Leonarda did, and it was enough to drive them to wailing despair.

Leonarda only had a moment to feel a little smug at the weakness of the others before the earthquake really hit. The earth beneath them rippled like water, throwing anyone who'd made it to their feet on the ground, but that nauseating motion was nothing compared to the hellish noise that echoed around the valley. As the stones of the hills bucked and cracked, so too did the man-made structures. But while the hills had the mass to survive being slung back and forth, bricks did not. In one great rippling line, the people in the fields watched the earthquake rip through their town, toppling walls, collapsing roofs, and flinging cobblestones from the road into the air and raining them back down like hailstones.

This was a doom like nothing Leonarda had ever seen. By moonlight, she saw the earth itself swallowing up the home she'd come to love and the life that she'd built along with it. She wondered if this was the madness that the fortune-tellers had warned her of or just the clearest sign yet that no matter where she went or what she did, the curse would pursue her and destroy all that she held dear. For long, agonising minutes, the roar of stone went on, and the town crumbled to dust. A few of the people who'd been asleep in their homes ran out, only to be knocked down by the rain of stone. The ones who fled for the forest or the river found that every natural landmark they'd known throughout their lives had been knocked aside by the heaving earth.

Then, just as suddenly as the chaos and destruction had begun, it stopped. The roar of stone, the heaving of the earth, the screaming of the terrified people — it all cut off abruptly, leaving an eerie silence in its wake, punctuated only by the clatter of stones and roof tiles raining back down.

When the screaming started again, it wasn't fear that dragged the guttural howls from the throats of the people still in town, but pain. For all the fury of the earthquake, there were still survivors trapped in the rubble of Lacedonia. Even the folk who didn't have friends and loved ones trapped in the ruins of their town rushed into the remains of their homes to try and retrieve whatever wealth could be salvaged. The only family that didn't were the Pansardis. Leonarda had struggled up from the ground onto her knees but had no strength to rise any further. The doom that she'd been waiting for had finally struck them down, taking everything from them and killing the town of Lacedonia in the process.

This was all her fault. All those people had died because she'd chosen to come here. Her dark fate had swallowed them all. Leonarda couldn't be moved, so Raffaele and the children stayed there with her, huddled around her. It was only her paralysis that kept them alive, which meant they hadn't gone back into the town before the aftershocks hit.

As many people that died when the earthquake first rolled through were killed when the aftershocks set all of the rubble back into motion. The people who were trapped in the ruined buildings were crushed; the survivors who were trying to save them died alongside them. The death toll of the 1930 Irpinia earthquake was a little over 1,400 people, almost all of them in Avellino, centred around the little town of Lacedonia. Every single home was destroyed by the time that the aftershocks had stopped a day later, and it would be 40 years before serious reconstruction of the town was finally undertaken.

For Leonarda, the psychological impact of the quake was almost as severe as the physical one. They'd lost their home, their livelihood, and all of their possessions, and while they found shelter in the shacks that the local government had thrown up for survivors, the truth was that their lives in Avellino were over. All of the stability and security that she'd wrapped around herself like a blanket had been stripped away in an instant by forces so powerful and unknowable that they may as well have been supernatural. Any doubts she'd ever been able to entertain about her curse being a figment of her imagination were wiped away along with the happy life that they'd so briefly known.

The Soap-Maker of Correggio

There were four living children left when all was said and done. Leonarda had lost 10 of them in childhood. All that was left were Giuseppe, two girls, and the youngest boy. Only they had survived earthquakes, epidemics of illness, and the arduous journeys across country to finally arrive with Leonarda and Raffaele in the quiet town of Correggio.

It was known throughout town that they were refugees of the terrible earthquake that had struck near Naples, and charity overflowed on their arrival. A clerical job was quickly found for Raffaele, and the family was able to rent a small house in the middle of town that had previously been attached to a general store. In a strange way, they'd landed on their feet. The kindness of the town soon turned into acceptance of the newest residents. The children were well-liked by the others their age, and now that Leonarda's doom had been unleashed so catastrophically, she no longer felt compelled to watch them every moment of the day. The earthquake had broken her of the idea that any intervention she could make would protect her babies.

It had broken her in more ways than one, though. She spent the first few weeks in Correggio staring into space, accepting the charity of the town but barely even acknowledging the women who were visiting with the parcels and baskets of gifts. None of these things mattered anymore. Not when everything could be stripped away in an instant for no reason at all.

She didn't believe in her new home. It was unreal to her. Everything was unreal to her except for the emotions that she was experiencing. When the numbness of her great trauma began to fade, the sense of building dread that had been pursuing her over the last few years had entirely vanished. She felt rage at all she'd lost, grief over the friends who'd died. The full range of human emotions was finally available to her, now that the shadow of anxiety had briefly abated. She didn't know what to do with all of the things she was feeling. She thought that she'd known relief when she gave birth to children without the red claw of miscarriage snatching them away, but each time, her anxiety had just built upon itself. Finally, there'd been some huge catastrophic outlet for the curse that hadn't left her with something new to worry about.

In Correggio, the family was solvent for the first time. They had savings and a home. All of the things that Leonarda thought she'd never get with her haphazard husband were finally coming to her. She wondered if the curse had spent itself destroying the town of Lacedonia. She wondered if she might finally be free. For the first time in her adult life,

Leonarda allowed herself to hope, and to dream of a better future.

In their first months in town, she'd been lying in her bed like a dead weight or going through the motions of motherhood, but now, for the first time, without the curse hanging over her, she felt like she could enjoy it. She laughed at her children's jokes. She smiled when her husband came home. Inexplicably, the earthquake seemed to have shaken away the patina of fear that had covered her, revealing the person that she was always meant to be. With the clarity of her new perspective, Leonarda seemed to realise how badly she'd been treating those around her, and she set out to make amends. Firstly, by doing all that she could to please her husband and children, and then by reaching out to the women of Correggio who'd offered them succour when they'd first arrived in town, to offer them long overdue thanks.

With her obvious mental illnesses, Leonarda had never been drawn into the social scene of the towns where they'd lived before, even if she did make a few friends everywhere that she went. But here, in Correggio, she finally got to experience the special bonds of friendship that only exist between large groups of women. She navigated the complex social tangles of small-town life with an expertise born of years dealing with her mother. She found herself embroiled in dozens of minor dramas without having any personal stake in any of them, and soon she found that the many women of the town were coming to her for advice, thanks to her presumed neutrality.

The imagination that she'd fought so hard to keep under control throughout all the years of anxiety now became an asset for the first time as she taught herself to write poetry.

Before long, she was sharing it with the other women of town during dinner parties and receiving standing ovations. She enjoyed the praise, but what really made her happy was when she overheard the other women of town talking about her. They talked about her poetry, her husband, her lovely children. Here in Correggio, free from the weight of her fears, she was spoken of with affection and respect. For the first time in her life, nobody was looking at her with contempt or pity. She was being treated just like everyone else.

Now that their immediate survival wasn't a concern and Leonarda felt like she was paying down the debts of gratitude that she owed, her attention began to spread further than the poems she was composing. Her children were getting older now. Giuseppe was practically a man in his own right. She had more and more free time on her hands with every passing day, and now, with some hope in her heart and a clear mind, she wanted to make use of that time.

Their home had been attached to a shopfront all the years that they'd lived in Correggio, but they'd kept themselves clear of the store, with the door through into that part of the building kept locked to stop the children roaming and to keep the heat of the hearth fire contained. Now Leonarda opened that door and stepped inside. There was a layer of dust and no shortage of cobwebs, but otherwise, the shop itself was intact. All that she'd need to start a business would be a product to sell.

It took her very little imagination to come up with soap. She'd learned how to make it during her tenure as a cleaner, many years ago, and she'd re-used her skills on an almost daily basis when keeping her home clean. With Raffaele's blessing, she ordered all of the perfumes and oils that she'd need to make her soaps special from the big city and set to work on her first batch.

A few short weeks later, she had the shop cleaned up, and Giuseppe was up on a ladder in the street painting the sign. The whole family and a choice selection of her new friends about town had tested her soaps and found them excellent, so much so that rumours had spread far and wide, and the whole town showed up for their grand opening. The shop was a roaring success, and soon news began to spread of the fine soaps that Leonarda Pansardi made. Requests started coming in from all over Italy as the news of her excellent products travelled far and wide.

It was success beyond her wildest dreams. The kind of fairy tale ending to her life story that she'd always hoped for, if she dared to hope. She was making enough money to support the family on her own now, enough to buy her children a fine apprenticeship and the certainty of a good future. Everything that she could've wanted was delivered to her on a silver platter. All thanks to a little bit of soap.

Despite all of this, she still found time to socialise with all of the women who'd made her acquaintance since their arrival in Correggio, inviting them to visit the shop for tea and cakes, while her daughter served the customers who were still flooding through.

Women still came to her looking for advice, but it was no longer because of her supposed impartiality in their disputes. During one of the many dinner parties that had run into the early hours of the morning, Leonarda had revealed her interest and training in the art of fortune-telling, and that had attracted a whole new kind of attention from the excitement-starved women of the town. When it became clear that the predictions that Leonarda had made when reading their palms were actually coming true, that once again shifted her position in the town's complex social hierarchy. She was soon being consulted, surreptitiously for the most part, by everyone of influence in the town. When a farmer had to choose what crops to plant, he came to ask the Soap-Maker. When a woman had to choose between two suitors, she came to ask the Soap-Maker. With her supposed oracular powers, Leonarda became the advisor to almost every adult in the town of Correggio, both to those who were superstitious enough to believe that she could predict the future, and to those who doubted her powers but believed that she must be terribly intelligent to successfully bilk everyone else in town into believing her patter. It seems likely that Leonarda, at least, believed in the veracity of her predictions, and she made statements during the readings that ran counter to her own best interests frequently enough that nobody suspected that she was using them as a means of manipulation.

Fame of her soap may have spread far and wide, but her fortune-telling remained a more localised open secret for the most part, although, when Romani caravans passed by town, they'd stop in at the store to buy her wares and share what stories they could of the outside world with Leonarda. It was as though they'd adopted her as one of their own.

These Romani visitors frequently brought Leonarda special gifts to offer in barter instead of buying her expensive and exquisite soaps outright. Books on the occult featured heavily in this trading, as did tarot cards, bone runes, and other paraphernalia of Italy's burgeoning spiritualist and mesmerist movements. Soon, she'd assembled a whole library of occult literature, comparable in scale to the ones boasted by many of the private collections that could be found, if one knew where to look in the biggest cities of Italy. This collection was her pride and joy, second only to Giuseppe, and as her interest in poetry waned, she began spending more and more of her evenings curled around those dark tomes, trying to unpick the nature of the curse that she believed had been set upon her.

Leonarda's reading soon strayed from her initial interest in palmistry and astrology into darker areas. At the time she began her studies, there were actually three separate forms of Italian folk magic being passed down by practitioners. The folk magic known as Stregheria was a modern offshoot of the older witch-cults that dominated the area before the rise of Christianity. In the '30s, anthropological studies had turned up a substantial amount of information on the history of the subject, but much of it was being subjected to the influence of a few editors with their own ideas on the subject before it made its way to print. As such, Stregheria more closely resembled the modern reconstruction religion of Wicca than the traditional practices of Italy.

Leonarda gathered those books and diligently read them, but they told her very little of the practical workings of the religion that they emulated. From those books, she branched out into other European witchcraft traditions, but because so much of the published materials were coming through the same publishers, they all had the same slant and the same lack of practical information.

She'd learn more about the two branches of traditional Italian folk magic by talking with its practitioners. The

Romani shared what they could, but through them, word spread to others with an interest in the subject, and soon, Leonarda had correspondents across Southern Italy in many unexpected places.

From these new friends, whom she knew only through letters, she learned about Benedicaria and Stregoneria. Benedicaria was the Tuscan traditional folk magic revolving around ancestor worship and household gods that stretched back to the Roman Empire, while Stregoneria was another modern re-invention of the traditional teachings disguised within the rituals of Catholicism in exactly the same way that Voodoo practitioners in the Americas concealed their practices under the same charade. From these paths, Leonarda began to piece together her understanding of magic, influenced in places by her studies of the Wicca-like Stregheria.

It wasn't enough for Leonarda to simply understand these subjects; she wanted to be an active participant in the rites and rituals involved in each of these niche religions. She wanted to be a fattuccchiere — a 'fixer' — stitching together brevi charm bags to work her will on the world, using herbs and spells to heal and hurt those around her. More than anything, she wanted to pick apart the threads of whatever curse was bound to her and set herself free once and for all. But to break a curse, she first had to learn how they were cast, and that took her into darker and darker territory in her studies. The books that she read soon needed translations and notes to be understood. The philosophical underpinnings of the rites and rituals gradually became clearer to Leonarda, and she began to practice as well as study, cooking extravagant meals on the equinoxes and performing spells in the privacy of her study when the working day was done.

For someone who'd lived her life at the whims of chaos, the idea of being able to control the flow of fate was terribly appealing, and even if the spells of protection that she wove over her family had no tangible effect in the real world, the psychological effect on her was pronounced. She'd learned to hope again in Correggio, treating it as an oasis in the inhospitable desert of her life, and now she felt that she had the tools to defend that peace. As long as she performed her rites and rituals, she believed that she could hold off whatever dark fate awaited her and her children.

As more of the town's people indulged in her fortune-telling, they soon learned of the other services that she could offer. When a girl found herself unexpectedly pregnant outside of wedlock, a trip down to see Leonarda would provide her with a tea of herbs that would strip the baby out. When a man found that he couldn't perform his duties as a husband, she'd have a mixture for him to swallow that would bring back his vigour. Even problems beyond health were soon being brought to the 'fixer' for an answer, and she stitched a good few dozen brevi through the years to create effects as varied as sickness, fertility, loyalty, and luck. Most popular were her spells of protection — the area where she'd poured the most of her time and study. She was possibly the greatest expert on Stregoneria protection rites in all of Italy.

All that she had to do now was to keep her head down, go through the rituals she'd learned, make her soap, and be happy. There was nothing more that could possibly go wrong.

In 1939, almost a decade after they'd arrived in Correggio and Leonarda had finally found some peace of mind, World War II broke out.

A Life for a Life

Mussolini's fascist party had been consolidating its control over Italy since 1922, transforming the nation into a totalitarian state within five years and then beginning a campaign of militaristic expansion that saw the invasion of Libya and Albania, the establishment of an Italian state in East Africa following the Abyssinian crisis, the carpet bombing of Corfu, and more covert efforts to spread Fascism around the world, including propping up Franco's coup attempt in Spain. Its goal was total domination, a return to the days of the Roman Empire, when Italy was the greatest power in Europe and, possibly, the world.

By 1939, the Italian position was precarious. Germany was its closest ally in the spread of fascism, and soon, they'd be launching their invasion of Poland, likely dragging that once proud nation's allies into a prolonged conflict. Italy had been invited to join Germany in a grand alliance with other Axis powers, but the military might that they could bring to bear was minimal after expending so much effort in their imperialistic expansions. Yet, they wouldn't withdraw from that alliance when they could see the potential prizes that were on offer. Accordingly, Mussolini began a desperate scramble to pump up the country's nationalism and recruit more soldiers. They had less than a year before war broke out — barely enough time to train soldiers in the basics before they could be flung onto the front lines.

All of his life, Giuseppe had been looking for a way to escape from his mother's shadow without hurting her. Her overbearing demands had always sat poorly with the boy, and without being privy to the full breadth of her madness, he couldn't help but look upon her with as much confusion as affection. He saw Leonarda as a fragile woman that he couldn't bear to hurt, but he also saw her as a terrible encumbrance. If it hadn't been for her, he might have had friends all his life instead of only, finally, being able to form relationships outside of his family for the first time when they arrived here in Correggio.

Joining the army presented him with the perfect excuse to slip through his mother's fingers in a manner that she couldn't possibly object to. Everyone in town was talking about how heroic the boys were for signing up to fight for Mother Italy. She would be proud of him. Her pride would overrule whatever irrational fears she might have about him joining up.

Propaganda was a science in its early stages back in the '30s, but Mussolini was an expert in its use. The general population of Italy, in particular, the young men, had been convinced that the coming war would be glorious and easy on them, that their enemies were weak and would be easily broken, just as the African nations that Italy had conquered had been. Italy may have had some indirect involvement in the Spanish Civil War, but the kind of direct combat that would be required to secure victory in World War II wasn't something that the individual man on the street might have had any sort of understanding about. They believed the state lies about the importance of their elaborate marching drills because they believed that all they would be doing was putting on a show of marching into the cities that they'd easily conquered.

Giuseppe had swallowed the party line without a second thought. Every young man has dreams of adventure, travel, and returning home a hero, but in the years of Mussolini's rule, it seemed that those dreams could become a reality as easily as signing on the dotted line. There were always military recruiters passing through every town, no matter how small the settlements were — they may very well have been the largest standing army in all of Italy's forces at the time. It was easy for Giuseppe to slip away while his mother was working, and he eventually put down his name.

In the years to come, recruitment would go from being an honour to being mandatory, but for now, Giuseppe got to ride on a wave of adoration from everyone in town as news of his noble decision spread. He enjoyed the attention, enjoyed being his own person for once instead of just 'Leonarda's son', but it did come with its downsides.

Leonarda had never made any effort to establish a good match for her eldest son, meaning that he was left to woo whichever girls in town were similarly unaccounted for. They weren't the cream of the crop, but Giuseppe made do, and before long, he had a shortlist of girls that he was entertaining quite regularly. None of them were strictly wife material, but they enjoyed his company, and him, theirs. Now that news had spread that he was going to be leaving town as soon as the levies were called, he seemed to lose his appeal for those girls. It made no sense to him — he'd just become the kind of heroic figure that they usually lost their minds over, and suddenly they no longer wanted him. It wouldn't be until later that he realised his biggest value to every one of the girls he'd been courting was as a potential husband, not as a partner they enjoyed spending time with.

The men may have swallowed all of Mussolini's lies about glories of battle, but the women of Correggio had a longer memory. World War I had been just a generation before, and they could all recall the husbands and sons who never came home. There were no graves for them, no statues or parades, just the cold artillery-peppered mud of Turkey. 600,000 Italian men had died in the Great War, and more than a million came home crippled for life. The sight of a man with no legs or a missing arm was so commonplace that those veterans had faded into the background of Italian life. But still, the women remembered, and they knew that Giuseppe had even odds of never coming home again if he went off marching with the other boys. There was no value in a husband who never came back.

The other obvious drawback of news travelling through the town grapevine was that, eventually, all news flowed to the woman behind the scenes of every decision that got made in the town: Leonarda.

For the first few days, he was safe, because nobody believed for a moment that he could've decided to sign up without telling his mother. Then, they were paralysed with indecision. Nobody wanted to be the bearer of such ill tidings. Eventually, Leonarda found out when she was walking to market, and she heard people calling out to congratulate her on her brave son. She didn't panic. In fact, it almost seemed as though she hadn't heard the news at all. She walked through Correggio as if she were in a trance, buying the things that she needed for dinner without a word or glance to any of the many people who greeted her warmly. It was like the shell-shock that had taken her after the earthquake almost a decade before had suddenly returned.

Once she arrived home, she laid out all of the materials for dinner and headed off to her study. Only once the door was locked, and she was certain that nobody might hear did she collapse in a wailing, weeping heap. All of this time, she thought that she'd kept darkness from their door. All of this time, she'd been certain that her rites and spells were enough, but now this. Now, her most beloved, firstborn son, was going to die, alone and in agony.

The women of Correggio hadn't forgotten the Great War, and now Leonarda was one of them. The horrors of the first war had passed her family by in her childhood, thanks to the social hierarchy that governed so much of Italian society, first because her mother's position was too elevated among the aristocracy and then because her father and step-father were beneath contempt. Still, it was impossible to live in the gutters of society and not see the other refuse drizzling down around you. She'd seen the cripples coming back to town expecting a hero's welcome and, instead, being treated like a burden. She'd seen so many women, grown plump on a soldier's salary, suddenly withering away at the arrival of an inevitable letter.

Her son. Her Giuseppe. He was no soldier. He couldn't even win the few fist-fights that his idiot friends had dragged him into through the years. If he went off to war, then he'd come home in a casket, if there was even enough of him to be scraped together. These were her rational concerns, the ones that any mother in the same position would share, but Leonarda didn't live in a rational world. Her world wasn't composed of logic; it was a darker and more chaotic place. Her world was composed of spells and curses, words and herbs that could heal or kill as the "Strega" demanded. In that world, there were no coincidences or bad decisions. There was only the will of Leonarda set against the power of a curse so powerful that it had destroyed an entire town the last time it flexed. All of her studies had been leading her to this moment. Fate had been leading her to this singular crisis point. Even the destruction of their life back in Lacedonia had just been a prelude to the battle that she'd now fight to save her son. Everything that she'd learned through her studies and dealings with the other Fattuccchiere had been learned to protect her precious, miraculous son from harm.

It would be the greatest magical working that she'd ever attempted, and it would take her days or weeks of study just to be certain of the metaphysical underpinnings of the spells that could save him.

When Giuseppe returned home that night, with almost a bottle of wine in his belly from all the toasts that had been raised to him in the tavern, the house was dark. All of the ingredients for a tasty meal had been laid out in the kitchen and forgotten, and even the hearth fire had burned away to ash. His younger siblings were nowhere to be seen, probably rescued by Raffaele and taken away to some little bistro when he realised that a meal wouldn't be forthcoming. He was alone in the darkness and silence, except the house wasn't silent, not completely. He could hear his mother's voice, speaking away softly. The turning of pages. The scratching of pen on paper. He crept through the house, nervous at what he might discover but certain that what he was imagining couldn't be worse. He'd lived through his mother at her worst when she was so wracked by terror that she wouldn't leave the house, and her own body betrayed her and cast her to the dirt. No matter what he found at the top of the stairs, it couldn't be as bad as what he'd previously witnessed.

This was his home, and he should have felt free to walk about it without this mounting sense of dread, but instead, he crept up the stairs as if there was a monster waiting for him behind the study door. His hands were shaking as he turned the handle and let the candlelight spill out. His mother was sitting at her desk, with her back turned to him. There were a half-dozen books laid out around her seat like the feathers of a peacock; ancient books in a half-dozen languages that he couldn't even begin to decipher. Her pen never stopped moving even as her eyes drifted from page to page, book to book. The incessant scratching was enough to raise his hackles. He reached out to touch her on the shoulder, and all at once, the writing stopped. She turned to face him with a beatific smile on her face. 'My darling boy. You're home.'

Together they shared a sparse meal of leftovers in the kitchen, the kind that they used to eat when she'd been so lost in her madness that she forgot to feed the children, but this time, it felt different to Giuseppe. It no longer felt like a disappointment, it was a childhood memory brought to life, and he found that he cherished it. His mother could've ranted and railed at him for sneaking off and joining the army without her say-so — most of the town wouldn't have even considered making a decision of that magnitude without consulting her first — but instead, she was talking to him like he was her equal instead of her child. He wondered if this was what adulthood and respect felt like, to sit at the table and make the decisions that set the course of lives.

Unsurprisingly, Leonarda wasn't in favour of him joining the army, but of course, he'd known that before he snuck off to do it. She'd always been so afraid that he might die that she never let him live, and this was no different. What did surprise him was how calmly she seemed to take the news. Secluding herself in her study all day and night hadn't been sane acts, yet now she walked him through all of the options available to him with all of the calm logic he'd always doubted she possessed. Was there any way for him to get out of serving in the army? Could he take back his consent? Was there any legal way that he might escape service? As they ticked each option off as impossible, he'd expected her to grow distraught, to tear out her hair and scream at him, but she didn't. She seemed almost resigned, like his leaving was a foregone conclusion that she had no chance of stopping, like she'd already accepted the new fate that he'd written for himself. It was more than he could have ever hoped for.

For Leonarda, it really was just a matter of going through the motions, finding out how long that she had, and searching for the missing component in the ritual that would grant Giuseppe the protection that he needed to survive the war and, more importantly, the curse. All of the times she'd been unreasonable with her son in the past had come from the belief that it was the only way to protect him. Now that his death was at hand, she found that all she wanted was for him to love her the way that he always should have, without the demands of misfortune that only she could predict weighing on their relationship. She'd moved beyond the emotional impact of the current problem and on to the practical solution.

Before Giuseppe had returned home, Leonarda had already hit upon the key point that all of the texts around death magic and warding against it agreed upon. Whether it was in the local Italian books or the more obscure texts from further afield, the only point that every different ritual agreed on was simple. It was a rule that had been codified in the forgotten study of alchemy, which had later been absorbed into dozens of different mystical traditions: the law of equivalent exchange. To get something, you had to give something of equal value. To save a life, Leonarda would have to give a life. That basic rule was just one cornerstone of the spell that she planned to work. There were two more factors that she hadn't worked out yet — the specifics of the rituals that would transfer the life from whoever she chose to take it from and how she could convey the protection onto Giuseppe. Her brevi bags were all well and good, but in the hustle and bustle of war, her boy could become separated from one all too easily. It wasn't enough to hand him her protection, she had to get it all over him, but inside him, if she could. She had to smother every inch of him in her protection if he was going to survive the curse.

It was good to be distracted, chattering away with him, just as it was good to be distracted thinking about the specifics of the rites she'd perform and pondering the method of delivery. All of these things were good because they kept her from having to think about the single act that would make the whole spell work. Murder.

Never in all of her life had Leonarda considered hurting someone else. There'd been the matter of fraud, but the only one who lost out when she took money from the pocket of the bank were the bankers, and they had more than enough money to get by. Leonarda didn't even like to hurt animals if she could help it, buying her chickens already plucked and butchered like she was some fancy lady. The sight of blood didn't trouble her too much — she'd been through too many miscarriages to give a spot of red too much thought — but the idea of causing something else pain was anathema to her. She'd suffered too much in her life to ever want to inflict the same kind of suffering on anyone else. Yet that was what fate demanded of her. Even after her talk with Giuseppe was done and they'd gone to their respective beds, even after Raffaele had returned home and snuggled up against her like some great dog with his master, she still lay there awake in the dark, staring up at the starlight-streaked ceiling and thinking about the thing she was going to have to do.

There were two sides to it. She wanted to make sure that the killing itself was as painless as she could make it, but she also wanted to make sure that she wasn't caught. If she killed someone and an uproar went up before she could complete her spell, then it was all for nothing. A life was wasted. That was even more terrible than a life that had been taken in the service of some greater purpose. There were so many pointless deaths in the world; she needed to be sure of her plans if she didn't want to add to them.

There were many herbs that could serve the first purpose, little remedies that could be overdosed to kill instead of heal. If all she wanted to do was snuff out a life at random, it would be almost effortless to give the next person that came wandering in looking for some cure or the wrong dosage and let them kill themselves. That would leave a body somewhere out in the town, and questions, and Leonarda didn't know how she would handle either. To keep things quiet, she needed to have full control over the situation, which meant that whomever she killed would have to die right here in the house.

It sickened Leonarda to think of polluting their home in this way, but there was nowhere else she could be certain that she wouldn't be disturbed, and nowhere else that all the other workings of the ritual would be so close to hand. It had to be done here in their home where she could conceal all signs of the killing with ease.

The nauseous feeling that these plans evoked in her were pushed down. She couldn't think about the morality of her actions or of the emotional impact that they might have on her. There were greater things at stake than her happiness and mental peace. The life of her son hung in the balance of her actions in these coming days.

Still, she made no action, nor even solid planning towards her killing. Not yet. There were still all the details of the ritual to work out and the medium by which she would imbue her protection upon Giuseppe. As long as those two problems remained, she didn't need to concern herself with the gruesome details of the murder.

Over the coming days, Leonarda spent all of her free time locked away in her study, piecing together the exact method by which her protection could be placed on Giuseppe. In part, she devoted so much time to those studies because it gave her an excuse to delay thinking about the other parts of her plan, but she was also obsessed with getting every single detail correct. She was only going to have one chance at this, so it had to go right.

Her entire life had been leading her to this moment. She knew that now. Everything that she'd experienced, everything that she'd learned, it had all been so that she could protect Giuseppe from the danger that was awaiting him. He'd been her miracle child. The one to beat the curse, first in her womb, then through his childhood. He was the first of her children that she'd consider having made it all the way to adulthood, and of course, he was the one with the biggest target painted on his back for the curse. All of her life, she'd been fighting against the curse, sometimes managing to hold it off for years at a time before it came back with a vengeance, but now, finally, she thought that she might be able to thwart it once and for all. If she could protect Giuseppe from the killing curse that had set its attention on him, then her lifetime of suffering might finally end. This could be the moment that let her break her mother's hold on her.

It was as she contemplated fate and her place in this continuum of events that the solution to one-third of her troubles clicked into place, at last. Soap and food. She would use soap and food as the joint mediums by which she would lay her protection on Giuseppe. She would protect him inside and out. It made perfect sense. Why else would she have learned how to cook and make soap, if not for this?

To understand the way that Leonarda made her decisions, it helps to have an understanding of extreme narcissism. Everyone in the world believes that they're the main character of their own story, to some degree, but for Leonarda, this wasn't just a general feeling of a life centred on herself — it was a genuine belief that everything that happened in the world was supernaturally governed by her. If things were going well, it was because she'd thwarted the curse that had been laid upon her. If it wasn't going well, it was because of supernatural forces that were arrayed against her. Every piece of evidence could be fed into this delusion, on one side or the other, to support her supposition. In much the same way that any evidence against a conspiracy theory can be discounted as evidence of the imagined conspiracy's ability to create misinformation, so did every event in Leonarda's life prove to her that she was the most important person in the world, and that all events revolved around the clash of will and magic between her and her mother. If all of this was true, then anything that Leonarda did to defeat her curse was morally justified. No matter how bizarre or depraved her actions were, they didn't matter because they were in the service of this greater good. Leonarda was the main character in her story, and everyone else in the world was a supporting character — they didn't have stories of their own, they didn't have dreams and hopes or struggles and despair. They were just playing pieces to be moved around in her own personal conflict. She was the only real person in the world, and only her story mattered. The fact that she chose to make her story one of martyrdom in the protection of her son was more to do with what she believed made for a good story rather than any sort of self-sacrificing nature that she might have possessed.

With the means by which she'd apply her spell resolved, the other elements of the ritual fell into place. It was like she'd found the jigsaw puzzle piece that all the rest of the picture attached to. She knew exactly how she would prepare her spell and how she would enact it. All that remained was the final part of her planning — the sordid business of planning and executing a murder, undetected.

Faustina Setti

Leonarda was in a position of absolute trust that any aspiring murderer would envy. Every day she had appointments scheduled with the women of the town, and the ones that came to her the most frequently were the ones who were the most alone and vulnerable.

Many of the town's women would come to Leonarda to discuss matters of love. She'd been instrumental in making many matches when it seemed that familial negotiations had broken down, thanks to her position as a neutral party and her unerring ability to pair the correct young people together to ensure good marriages. Even outside discussions of romance, the spinsters of the town were more frequent visitors to her shop thanks to their greater desire for social interaction. Times weren't easy for unwed women, and while the Great War had made many widows, they at least had the consolation of their children and pensions. This was still long before even the first hints of women's liberation crept into provincial life. Without a man to govern her, a woman had no social standing to speak of. It was believed that women were incapable of making decisions for themselves, so when a married woman did so, it was seen as an extension of her husband's will. Likewise, with a young woman and her father. The fear of bringing shame on their family and, more specifically, the patriarch of that family, was often sufficient to curb any reckless tendencies that they might have. Even widows, who often ended up as the ruling matriarchs of whole dynasties of Italian families, were often viewed as merely enacting the will of their expired husbands, doing as he would've done in the circumstances — which made the spinsters into an uncomfortable anomaly. Adult women capable of choosing their own course through life ran contrary to the common wisdom, so people didn't know how to deal with them. They became pariahs within their community, shunned by men and mostly overlooked by other women. It was a half-life, intended as a subtle warning to women that if they didn't behave in the manner that was desired, if they didn't present themselves at all times as marriage material, then the kindnesses that were afforded to them could be withdrawn just as easily. Spinsters were the subject of ridicule and the punchlines of jokes, beneath contempt.

Out of all the women in Correggio, none had been the butt of more jokes and suffered the undercurrent of disrespect more frequently than Faustina Setti. All through her life, Faustina had been unlucky in love. Marriage arrangements that had seemed concrete fell through, and opportunities for courting seemed to dry up as the years progressed. There were very few unmarried men left in the town of Correggio, and the vast majority of the ones that hadn't settled down were unmarried for a very good reason. Even knowing this, Faustina had still pursued the majority of them to the natural end of their potential relationships. It was these futile attempts at romance that first brought her to Leonarda's door, seeking advice, and it was only by taking that advice that she'd managed to avoid the myriad tragedies that each of the awful men she'd set her heart on would've brought her. To be single through your twenties was an embarrassment, through your thirties, a travesty. But for Faustina to be alone through her forties too was monstrous. It meant that she'd be alone forever, living half a life, for her entire life. She still desired an escape from her life of solitude, and she'd been coming to Leonarda for over a year, begging her to find a suitable partner for her to live out her later years with.

Despite all of the powers that the town's women had ascribed to her and all of the studies that she'd made into the art of divination, Leonarda hadn't been able to grant this lonely woman's wish. This, like so many other things, Leonarda would now blame on fate. It wasn't Faustina's fate to be wed. It was her fate to serve a far higher calling than mere matrimony. She'd gone all of her days a blessed virgin so that her soul would be pure when it passed on to the next life. The life she gave would provide all of the protection that sweet, innocent Giuseppe would require.

When Faustina next came to visit Leonarda, she found the woman to be possessed of an almost manic energy. The energy was infectious. Almost as soon as the door had closed behind Faustina, Leonarda grasped her hands and told her the one thing that she'd been waiting for all of her life to hear. 'I've found you a husband.'

Faustina was practically vibrating out of her seat by the time that Leonarda had made the tea and settled across the table from her. Before Leonarda could even open her mouth, the woman blurted out, 'Who is he?'

The story that followed was sparse on details but rich on the kind of ornamentation that Leonarda usually threw into her grandest predictions of the future. There was a man in Pola — the country that would later become a part of Croatia — who'd seen Faustina's picture and fallen in love. Leonarda had been sending letters to him on Faustina's behalf, and at last, the arrangements for the marriage were to be made. All of Faustina's dreams were coming true.

Arrangements here in Correggio would need to be advanced before the wedding could go ahead. Faustina passed all of her life savings over to Leonarda, to arrange her safe passage to her new home, and in turn, Leonarda gave her some important advice. She was taking a step into the unknown, and the people who loved her might fear that unknown. Even though this was the only true path to happiness, they might try to stop Faustina because they couldn't see where the path ended. The element of surprise was going to be essential if Faustina wanted to make it to her new life in Pola, but that didn't mean that she should abandon all of her friends.

Leonarda explained exactly what should be done. Faustina needed to write a letter to each of her friends, explaining that she was travelling to Pola to meet her new husband and start her life anew. She should include all the assurances that each of her family members would need and describe a safe and happy journey. Leonarda would then arrange for each of these letters and postcards to be sent to the recipients over the coming weeks to simulate Faustina's safe journey. When

Faustina asked why she couldn't simply send real letters, Leonarda explained that the mail service had been spotty, and she didn't want any of Faustina's friends to worry. More importantly, Leonarda had already foreseen the safe and comfortable journey that Faustina was going to be describing. All that she had to do was write the letters and come back to Leonarda's house the following morning with her travel bag packed.

It was barely dawn when Faustina arrived, and Leonarda had to drive the rest of her family out of the house so that she could get to business. The manic and erratic edge to her behaviour would've unsettled Faustina normally, but today of all days, she was feeling just as overwrought. The life that she'd known was going to be a thing of the past. She was journeying off into the unknown to start a new life with a man that she'd never met before, but whom she was certain would be the love of her life. She was certain of her course, but that didn't mean she wasn't a jangling ball of nerves.

Leonarda looked on her friend fondly, put an arm around her shoulders, and guided her to the kitchen table. 'Sit and calm yourself. All will be well soon enough.' She brought over a decanter and poured out a glass of wine. 'For your nerves.'

Faustina took it gratefully, despite the earliness of the hour, and took a long slurp of the bitter, herbal red. It did seem to calm her. Leonarda was sitting across the table from her with an unwavering smile fixed on her face. 'Go on, drink up. It'll help.'

With a little giggle, Faustina finished off her drink with a toss of her head, the last grainy dregs of sediment slipping back down the side of the glass. The wine tasted herbal and bitter, not at all like the sweet red it had been when she took her first sip. Leonarda wasn't saying anything at all, just staring at her. Even her breathing seemed to have stopped. So early in the day, with all of the people in the house gone, it was almost eerily quiet. Usually, when Faustina visited, there was the hustle of people being served through in the shop, the bubbling of soap being made, and the soft undercurrent of conversation, but right now, there was dead silence.

'Leonarda?'

The dawn seemed to be reversing, the light pouring in through the east-facing windows was growing dim and red. Faustina tried to turn and look outside to see the sun going back down, but her movements were languid and sluggish. She couldn't convince her body to move the way that it should. When she tried to say something to Leonarda, the words wouldn't come. Her tongue sat like a salted slug in her mouth. When she forced her head to turn back to Leonarda, she discovered that the other woman wasn't there. Her seat sat empty.

The wine glass loomed large in Faustina's vision. The sediment looked like some mix of herbs and powders, poorly blended. Modern drugs and Leonarda's herbal cures. All together. All freezing her in place. Her head lolled back as muscular control escaped her, and that was when she saw her friend one last time. Leonarda had gone out of the room to fetch an axe. Why would she need an axe? There was no wood to split, and the stove was already fully stocked. It must have been. Why else would the kitchen feel so very warm?

Leonarda was coming towards her with the axe. She was speaking, but the drugs were making it too difficult for Faustina to concentrate. She couldn't understand a word. It was like Leonarda was chanting in some foreign language.

Somewhere between the woman entering the room with the axe and closing the distance, candles had flickered to life around them. The heat from the oven and the glow of the candles had Faustina slick with sweat. It was running into her eyes and stinging them, but she couldn't wipe it away or force her eyes shut. She had to sit there and watch as Leonarda strained to heft the axe above her head. The rush of adrenaline, when she realised what was happening, must have been enough to snap everything back into focus, because she understood the last thing that Leonarda said before she brought the axe down. 'Sorry.'

Leonarda's first strike missed its mark. She wasn't strong enough to wield the axe well as a weapon, and she'd been passing off the duty of splitting logs to her husband since they were married. It had always been his job, never the children's. The curse and her dark fate followed blood, not marriage. She could trust him not to cut himself or send splinters of wood into his own eyes. Raffaele could always be relied upon to survive.

She tried to keep her mind on him, on her son, on anything other than what she was doing right now. She tried to breathe through her mouth so that the stench of voided bowels and blood couldn't reach her. It crept into her mouth all the same. She could taste the iron tang on the air. It took all her strength to pull the axe from where it had wedged in Faustina's shoulder. She couldn't look at her friend's face. That was why she'd missed with her first swing. She could not think of Faustina at all. If she did, then she would falter. It would all be for nothing if her will was broken. The body before her was making a high-pitched whine. Despite the copious amounts of blood soaking out into her clothes, Faustina was still alive, still conscious, despite the drugs.

Her eyes were pleading when Leonarda met them, wet with tears but still dreadfully full of life and awareness. This time, Leonarda didn't flinch away; she didn't turn her face from the sight of what she'd done. She brought the axe down on the centre of her friend's head.

Weakness prevailed again, regardless of Leonarda's intent. Instead of punching through Faustina's skull, the axe blade deflected on the bone. It turned, shearing away scalp and face in a great, gory mess. The whine grew in intensity.

There was no way out but through. Leonarda swung the axe again and again. Pieces of Faustina fell onto the tile floor. Chunks of meat and bone. There was so much blood. It felt like Leonarda might drown in it. Her face was soaked by arterial spray, her tears cutting tracks down through it as she hacked at Faustina's body again and again.

The whine continued, trilling in Leonarda's ears as she swung again and again. Why wouldn't Faustina stop? Why wouldn't she just die? There were four separate pieces of her on the floor already. How could she still be screaming? Even as Leonarda wondered, the screaming seemed to get louder, and her chopping more frantic. It took a long minute before she realised that she was the one doing the screaming now.

The axe tumbled from her hands to land on the floor with a splash. Faustina was dead, and Leonarda's kitchen was a charnel house. She would've collapsed there and then, exhausted both physically and mentally, but if she did, then it would all be for nothing. She could already picture Raffaele's face when he walked into the home of their family and took in this sight. Leonarda had been warned what would happen to her if she faltered in her path — in one hand, prison, in the other, the asylum. Which one would her husband condemn her to if he found her like this?

With leaden limbs, she began to move forward. Not out of fear of the injustices she would suffer if she stopped here, but because her work wasn't yet finished. If she faltered now, then the death would be in vain. If she faltered now, then Giuseppe would die, too. She had to keep going. Now that Faustina was dead, draining the remaining blood from the body was the first step. Leonarda hung the body parts from herb-drying hooks and let them drain into basins. The rest of the blood, she began to mop away. The floor was clean, but not clean enough that she could trust the blood wasn't contaminated with other particulates. She couldn't have the workings of her spell spoiled by a smudge of dirt. There was too much at stake.

Each piece of flesh had to be carefully worked and massaged to draw all of the blood out. It was the blood that would form the basis of the protection Giuseppe would carry inside himself. Leonarda cursed herself for spilling so much of it in vain. By the time that the pieces were pale and empty of blood, she barely had a basin full, and half the day was gone.

She emptied the blood into trays and slid them into the roasting hot oven that she'd spent all night stoking. In the oven, the blood would dry out and become a workable ingredient for the rest of the spell, and Leonarda's time wouldn't be wasted while it did. She took the pieces of Faustina, now as dry as she could make them, and placed them in pots of caustic soda, the same compound that she used to render fat into soap. It was powerful enough to dissolve every single part of the dead woman that was leftover, from her hair to her bones. With a scarf wrapped around her face to hold back the fumes, Leonarda heated and stirred the great pots on the stove where she cooked her family's meals.

From then, it was just like any other day for Leonarda. She prepared the ingredients for teacakes. She rendered down the fat until it was a gruesome brown, tinged soup, simmering and hissing. She hummed a little song to herself as she went through the motions. It could've been any other day in her kitchen.

When she drew the trays from the oven, there was a thin rust-coloured coating along the bottom of each. She had to scrape it off into the bowl with the flour, sugar, and eggs. With everything else in the teacakes, she didn't expect Giuseppe to taste anything awry, but to be sure, she added a sprinkle of vanilla to the mix. She couldn't taste any difference when she bit into the first of them, but her nose had been full of the reek of death all day. She felt like, no matter how she scrubbed, she'd never be clean again. That was only right. She should bear the weight of her sins. She deserved to feel that way. She'd sinned.

There was only a small mirror in the kitchen, but she studied herself in it thoroughly to make sure that the gore coating her face was purely imaginary. The weight of her sins she could bear, but the weight of the consequences, if anyone found out about this human sacrifice, were too much to tolerate. She'd scrubbed every trace of blood from her kitchen floor, from the tables and counters, from the walls and the ceiling. Her clothes were changed and soaking in vinegar to break up the blood. Everything in the kitchen looked as it always had. It was as if nothing had happened at all.

Even the pots bubbling away on the stove were a familiar sight and sound. It calmed Leonarda's heart for everything to be back to normal. It reassured her that life could go on even though she'd done this terrible thing to save her son. It took some effort, but she finally managed to draw a normal breath again. The frenzy that had taken her since she first slipped poison into the wine decanter — now also thoroughly cleaned out — was beginning to fade. Her hands shook now as the adrenaline that had been driving her forward all day subsided, and the edges of her vision began to darken. It was like she'd been possessed until the act was done. Possessed by the greater purpose that, even now, was fleeing her body.

It was nice to sink back down into her own humanity, to forget the thing that she'd become for those dreadful hours of gruesome work. She could feel all of that nervous energy seeping out of her, leaving the dull ache of a long day's hard work behind. By the time that the pots would normally have been done dissolving away solids, Leonarda was herself again, calm and happy that her goal had been achieved. She had to remember that it was all worthwhile, that it was all for Giuseppe. She lifted a lid off one of the pots to check on the progress, and it tumbled from her suddenly numb fingers. Filth. Sludge. Slime. It wasn't even close to being right to make soap. It was vile fluid, corrupted and sickly. Something had gone wrong. In all of her experiments comprised of meat, bones, and cut hair over the last few months, it had never produced a foul ichor like this. She wouldn't dare to make it into soap and rub it on her precious son. It was vile. The rite had failed. She'd failed. It had all been for nothing.

She emptied the pots into buckets, marched them to the nearest septic pit, and poured them in. It was a fitting end for a wasted life. She didn't weep for Faustina. She wept for her son. Her failure would kill him.

Francesca Soavi

It took weeks before Leonarda could even contemplate where her spell had gone wrong and how it could be corrected. The trauma was still too fresh. But even though she couldn't commit to changing things in her grand plan yet, she still kept the figurative plates spinning. She entertained the other women who were potential victims. She performed as though she were any other woman in the community, and acted just as surprised as the rest about the sudden and romantic disappearance of Faustina to go and meet her new husband in Pola. Nobody knew how she'd met him, but the letters that Giuseppe had diligently posted from the next town over had done the trick perfectly to assuage any suspicions.

The family and visitors ate the teacakes, finding them crunchy but, otherwise, unremarkable. The tint of iron in their composition was overlooked. But despite the blood, they held no power to protect anyone. Only when the whole ritual was complete, and the protection was applied from every direction, could the teacakes do their work. They served their purpose for now — they made it so that Giuseppe would eat the little snacks without question, and they disposed of the last scraps of evidence that Leonarda had lying around the house.

Her rites and rituals had been perfect. She was certain of it. All of the research and reconstruction work that she'd done to ensure that her spell would protect him had been flawless. She dug back into her books, and in the end, the only conclusion that she could come to was that the exchange hadn't been equal. It was the only explanation. The life of Faustina, sad and shrivelled as it was, couldn't compare to the glorious future that Giuseppe had in store for him. For the exchange to work, she'd need a younger victim. She couldn't give her son just a few scarce years culled from the end of a lifetime of suffering. She needed to do more, give him more. After all, he had a whole life still to lead.

In August of 1940, just three months before the recruiter was due to come back through town and collect Giuseppe, Leonarda felt the pressure of necessity returning. She was running out of time. If she didn't try again and get it right this time, there'd be nothing to keep her son safe in the war. With a renewed appreciation for the value of the lives of her potential victims, Leonarda began the process of selecting her next target.

Francesca Soavi was a school teacher in Correggio for many years, retiring early to care for her sickly husband until his death. She was younger than Leonarda, and her life had been rich with joys as well as despairs. She had no children, so there was nobody specific to worry about her, but she was well-liked by the people of the town. Her husband's long illness had taken its toll on the family finances, and she now found herself destitute and her previous role at the local school filled. She needed to find work, but she had no idea how to go about it. These weren't the days of job-hopping. Most people stepped into a role and remained in that career for life. Women were typically excluded from that cycle, so there was even less of a support system for them than there would've been for a man who found himself unemployed later in life.

It was acknowledged that some jobs, by necessity, must be done by women, but even so, there was an undercurrent of discomfort in any interaction with these working women. They possessed a level of independence that didn't align with society's expectations of them. So, when she came to Leonarda with her sad story of a lost love and destitution on the horizon, it seemed obvious that what she really needed wasn't her fortune told or the gentle comfort that Leonarda typically offered people that their decisions were the correct ones. What she really needed was for someone to help her slot back into that working life on the periphery of acceptable society. She didn't need direction; she needed a connection. So that was what Leonarda promised her.

The routine was practically the same as her first victim. Leonarda learned what her victim wanted most in the world and then used it to bait the hook. She fed Francesca a story about a job working for an elite girl's school in Piacenza, in the northwest, towards Switzerland. It was a clever move. It was a university town with a host of international schools nearby, dotted around the mountains. Music, art, and philosophy were taught to the children of ambassadors, dignitaries, and royalty. These were the kind of places that couldn't afford to publicly advertise their location and invite people in for a casual job interview.

Letters of recommendation penetrating the layers of social strata would've been just the start. Yet that was exactly what Leonarda was able to offer Francesca. She still remembered enough of her mother's dalliances with high society to mimic their mannerisms. It was simple enough to convince Francesca that her client list extended into nobility and beyond, which was true, albeit in reference to her soap business rather than her fortune-telling, as she implied.

With the ghost of the mysterious school's authority hanging over her, it was even easier to manipulate Francesca into accepting secrecy than it had been Faustina. The very same postcards and letters were written ahead of time and delivered into Leonarda's hands and, finally, on the 5th of September, 1940, Francesca was ready to depart, and Leonarda had her spell workings ready.

It was early in the morning when Francesca arrived with her packed trunk bulging. She wasn't nearly as giddy as Faustina had been, but she was still nervous enough to accept the drink that was pressed into her hands.

As the room began to spin, she almost toppled off her chair before Leonarda's steadying hands were there to hold her in place. 'Rest easy.'

Drugged and confused, Francesca couldn't grasp what was happening. Had some sickness suddenly taken her? A stroke, like her husband had suffered? Leonarda was speaking to her softly, murmuring some comforting old song that Francesca could barely recognise the shape of. There were hands smoothing over her chest and her arms, digging under her coat and seeking out her pocketbook. Through the haze of sedation, she watched Leonarda pick her pocket and count out the lire she'd been saving for the trip. It was a pittance compared to the amount she'd stolen from her last sacrifice, but Francesca would have no use for it where she was going.

There was no frenzy this time when Leonarda fetched the axe. No wildness unleashed. Everything was methodical. Basins were laid out to catch every drop of the blood. Francesca's belongings were stripped off and secreted away alongside Faustina's cases. Leonarda lined herself up carefully for a killing blow from the very beginning. Then she swung.

The axe bit deep into the side of Francesca's head, and the blood began to cascade down to rattle into the metal basins. In itself, it would've been a killing blow, but Leonarda still had to divide the body, and she was certain that draining it of blood would be easier if it were in parts. The head, torso, and limbs were separated from each other, not as a surgeon would divide them, but as a butcher would hatchet cuts of meat apart for roasting, with gristle and broken bone showing in each gelatinous wound. There was a yellow layer when Leonarda wiped the blood away — a coating of fat hidden beneath the skin that had been missing from the scrawny Faustina. Maybe this was what she'd been missing? Not years, or dignity, or any other abstract. Maybe it had always been an issue of flesh and chemistry instead of mysticism. Leonarda set that thought aside as she strung up the pieces. It mattered little whether the fault was in Faustina's body or her spirit. She'd been delivered to Leonarda in her entirety, and a fault in any part of her was just a sign that fate did not approve of the offering that was being made. The perpetual danger of her obsessive fatalism was that any event, however unrelated, always came back to the same root cause — a force so far beyond the comprehension of a normal mind that it was entirely alien.

Francesca's blood drained easily from her remains. Her body parts broke down smoothly in the caustic soda. Order prevailed over chaos, just as Leonarda prevailed over fate. Every baking tray was filled with blood to the rim. The pots on the stove bubbled away smoothly. Even Leonarda herself needed only a quick clean off before she looked entirely normal. This time, it was going to work. She was certain of it. It was her haphazard panic that had spoiled things last time. Her erratic behaviour had soured the death and robbed it of meaning. She could recognise the fault in her actions now that she'd seen a sacrifice made correctly. This death wouldn't be for nothing.

The teacakes that Leonarda made this time had a distinctive iron bite to them. It set her teeth on edge, like she was charged with static electricity. It was the spell. It had to be the spell working. There was no other explanation. This time, Leonarda's horror had been subsumed by her excitement. She'd finally achieved her goal. She was still grinning when she lifted the lid off the pot and saw the unusable slop inside. Throughout her life, Leonarda had spoken often of curses, so it should be no surprise that she let one slip past her lips now. In a fury, she grabbed onto the nearest pot, intent on flinging it across the room, but before she could, the handles seared the palms of her hands, and she leapt back, yelping. She was being punished. Looking down at her hands, she could see the marks that this work had put on her. Her lifeline was bisected by the line of blistering skin on her palms, divided neatly in half into the time before this moment and the time after. The awful things that she was doing had left their mark on her, and the message couldn't be clearer. This was the turning point. This was when everything would change. Her new fate had been burned into her.

She had to wait until Giuseppe came home to get the contents of her pots dumped into the septic pit. A batch of soap gone bad. It happened, sometimes. Something wrong was mixed in with the fat that spoiled the result. It didn't even cross Giuseppe's mind to look at the slurry he was dumping out. All of his concern was with his mother. Even with bandages, she found she couldn't lift the pots, and it was a minor injury in the long run, but it still spoke to her deteriorating mental state that she was trying to grab at pots without towels to protect her hands from the heat. Giuseppe would have to keep a closer eye on his mother. He knew that she was upset about his plans to leave, but he didn't think that she would go as far as to hurt herself just to prove that she needed him to stay and take care of him. It was a level of crass manipulation that he'd thought she was better than, but apparently not.

He'd have to start paying closer attention to what his mother was up to. If he caught her in a lie once, it would be enough to break her out of whatever deranged cycle she was diving into, but if she continued unattended, then there was no telling how far she might go. She'd never shown any sort of self-destructive streak in the past — quite the opposite. She was so risk-averse it was sometimes difficult to get her to leave the house. Giuseppe understood that the decision he'd made was going to be a catalyst for change, but he'd never suspected that it might have so profound an impact on his mother's mental state. He'd never considered that the attention she lavished on him compared to his siblings was an indication of any underlying problem. The firstborn son was always the apple of his mother's eye, so it never even occurred to him that the disproportionate amount of time and effort that she'd invested in him was anything out of the ordinary.

He ate the teacakes she foisted on him when he came home and watched her potter around the kitchen, cleaning up the mess she'd made. The way that she told the story, her injury was just the result of absent-mindedness, but there was something false in the way that she said it, something guilty.

Outside of the bubble of Leonarda's protection, events on the world stage had been moving forward rapidly. World War II was now in full swing, and Italy had officially signed a non-aggression pact with Germany in June of 1940. France had been taken by Germany without Italian support, denying Mussolini much of the territory that he'd desired to claim. Opportunity felt like it was slipping through his fingers, so he committed Italy fully to the war from that point on.

While they had a hand in several minor conflicts elsewhere, much of Italy's efforts were spent in the North African theatre. War was gradually creeping closer and closer to the home front. By July, an indecisive battle between the British and Italian navies had been conducted just off the western coast. Correggio was far from all this, in landlocked Reggio Emilia, but Leonarda heard all through her network of likeminded friends across the country.

Despite this creeping encroachment, it seemed that the war was going well for Italy. They'd won several decisive victories in Africa, seizing great swathes of British-controlled territory and driving Allied forces out of the area. Mussolini was beloved by Hitler above all of his other pseudo-allies for these decisive victories, and the Germans upheld the Italians as their equals, giving the country its most powerful position on the world stage since unification. It wouldn't be long before the formal alliance of the Axis powers would follow.

Giuseppe followed the news just as closely as his mother, listening in on her conversations when he could, to garner the details that had been lost in the wash of patriotic propaganda. Even the eternal pessimist, Leonarda, couldn't convince herself that Italy was going to lose the war. No matter how many times she consulted her cards or interrogated her correspondents, she just couldn't foresee how the war was going to go against them.

Now that the war was actually in play, Giuseppe was spoiling to join the fight. Before, he'd made his plans to escape from his mother's influence as the guiding directive, but now, he was becoming caught up in the propaganda machine's never-ending churn. This was his chance to become a hero. He began quietly making plans to head into a bigger town and join up with his regiment earlier than was scheduled — plans that inevitably trickled back to Leonarda.

Time was running out, and she'd failed yet again in her attempts to protect Giuseppe. Something had gone wrong with the spell again. It wasn't a matter of chemistry, but of magic. She was certain that something was wrong with the spell, and that was why the soap was failing to form correctly.

It took her almost a full month of study before she worked it out. She'd approached both of her victims with the wrong intent, focusing entirely on the event at hand instead of the larger meaning of her actions. Even though she hadn't been lost in her emotions during the slaying of Francesca, her mind had still been on other matters — the mechanical performance of her task, rather than the rituals and rites that she should've been performing. Magic, as she'd learned it, was all about intent. Through intent, the Fattuccchiere communicated to the universe at large what changes she wanted to make, and by muddying that intent by focusing on the physical aspects of the sacrifice, Leonarda had spoiled the working of her will on reality. She had time for only one more attempt before Giuseppe slipped through her fingers and into the maw of death. This time, she wouldn't hesitate, and her will would be done.

Virginia Cacioppo

For her final victim, Leonarda had set her heart on the only other woman in town who could even compare to her own celebrity status. Virginia Cacioppo was a former soprano who'd sung at such famous opera houses as La Scala in Milan. She was known on sight throughout the town of Correggio and adored by the locals in equal measure to that visibility. Compared to the rather rural existence of the natives, she carried with her a cosmopolitan history that went beyond her fine clothes, perfumes, and mannerisms and into her education and bearing. She could hold conversations with the men of town without deference, and they listened to her opinion and gave it all of the weight that even Leonarda's years of ingratiating herself couldn't grant her.

There was no small amount of jealousy in the way that Leonarda looked at Virginia Cacioppo. If her life had taken a different course, if she hadn't been so intent on choosing her own husband, then it was possible that she could've ended up in a similar place in society. She had the same good breeding as Virginia, yet here she was making soap and being ignored, while Virginia did nothing and received standing ovations. Yet she couldn't bring herself to feel much anger towards Virginia because the woman was relentlessly polite and kind to everyone that she met.

She'd first come to the soap shop as a customer, but in no time at all, Leonarda found herself considering the other woman to be a friend. With her poetry and Virginia's singing, they were two creative souls in a town composed predominantly of artless philistines. They sipped fine wines and shared gossip from far away, and, for a while, Leonarda could forget her own life and slip into the dream that this genteel companionship was her reality. Virginia came to rely on Leonarda for advice, first in navigating the oddities of living in a small town, but soon, for everything. She'd learned about Leonarda's fortune-telling from the other women of the town and complained that she'd been quite bereft of spiritual guidance ever since she left the Opera. It was only natural that Leonarda should step up and clothe her regular advice in the garb of premonition. It was what she did for almost everyone else in town, anyway, reserving her genuine attempts at divination for when there were matters that went beyond the bounds of common sense.

It was a very pleasant feeling to be trusted and relied on by a woman like Virginia. It made Leonarda feel important. Their close association also made Leonarda more popular. As much as she'd been appreciated as a poet when she'd first arrived, her occult obsessions and insular nature had made her something of a social pariah in later years. Being around Virginia had reversed that decline, and Leonarda found her evenings filled with candlelit dinner parties, once more. It was easy to imagine the hand of fate at work in putting the two of them together. Both of them so far from where they'd first started out, in both geography and station, yet both of them drawn together across that great distance to meet here in Correggio.

When Virginia abruptly confessed to her that she planned to leave town, it felt like a betrayal. They were in this together, and now Virginia was going to escape on a whim? She had no plans or prospects, but the savings that Virginia had been living off were running out, and she couldn't rely on the charity of her brother for much longer. Her time in Correggio was drawing to a close, whether she wanted it to or not. There was nothing even resembling appropriate work for her in this little town. She had to leave, but she had no idea where to go. That was when she turned to her dear friend Leonarda for guidance.

Leonarda managed to temporarily delay her with a promise that she'd find a suitable prospect for her, but the whole time, the vicious clockwork of her mind was spinning. If Virginia left town, then the precious moments where Leonarda could pretend to be living the life she'd been meant to live, before her mother twisted up her fate, would be lost forever. It would be as if Virginia were dead. She might as well be dead.

Virginia was a special, wonderful woman. Of this, there could be no doubt. The kind of person whose life would have particular meaning. Someone touched by fate and drawn to Leonarda from across Italy.

The final pieces of the puzzle clicked into place for Leonarda. The law of equivalent exchange applied in all things. To save the remarkable life of an important person like Giuseppe, she would have to sacrifice someone who had equal value to the universe. Someone special. She'd been choosing her victims carefully, selecting those who were beneath the notice of society at large. That had been the flaw in her reasoning. Such meaningless women could never be worth as much as her precious Giuseppe. Virginia mattered to the world, and more importantly, she mattered to Leonarda. There was no value in her previous sacrifices because they meant nothing to Leonarda — they were just women that she happened to know, women who happened to be vulnerable. Virginia was different. When she died, Leonarda would mourn the loss. It would injure her to kill Virginia, and that pain was the fuel her magic needed. Killing some nobody wasn't a fair trade for saving Giuseppe, but killing someone that she would spend the rest of her life missing seemed closer to an equal exchange.

She made her preparations as she had for the last two, but this time, she made no attempt to shield her heart from the grief and anguish that she was feeling. In her way, she loved Virginia, and killing her would be the hardest thing that she'd ever had to do, and this time, there was no shying away from the act. There was no retreating into fantasy or pretending that the gruesome things that she had to do weren't happening. For the spell to work, she had to feel it as deeply as Virginia would feel the fall of the axe.

Baiting the hook was more complex this time. Virginia was not nearly as isolated or desperate as the first two women had been, and convincing her to leave without telling her brother was nigh on impossible. Leonarda had to be subtle this time, building her story and her demands up in layers.

To begin with, she informed Virginia that she'd found a job that would be suitable for her talents and station, but she couldn't share any details. Her secrecy just made the whole thing more appealing to the romantically minded Virginia. She loved the mystery of the whole process, and she took to pry details out of Leonarda every time that they met as though it were all some grand game. In a sense, it was, but she never knew that the stakes were her life. With time, she convinced Leonarda to tell her more, always on the condition that she'd keep everything that was divulged a secret. Day by day, she drew the details out. The job was secretarial. Virginia would be managing the household and business affairs of a working man. The job was related to the arts, so her background in the theatre would be an essential component. The work would involve the kind of parties and socialising that Virginia had once considered being her second nature, drinking and dancing with other famous people, and making connections that could be exploited later by her employer. The job was to the south. The job was in a big city. She'd be working for an impresario — one of the wealthy financiers who kept the Italian artistic scene afloat, putting up the money to have operas, art shows, ballet, and all of the rest displayed. They were the vanguard of culture, keeping the lights of civilisation on in these decidedly uncivil times. She'd be managing several establishments that this impresario held stock in, managing several bright, new stars on the rise. She may even be able to return to her training and do some singing herself. The impresario had heard of her. He was most interested to see if she might be returned to the stage where she belonged. The impresario lived just outside of Florence. She would have an apartment in

Florence when she started her work so that she could be at the heart of the thriving musical scene in the city.

It was a trail of breadcrumbs, leading Virginia further and further down the dark and winding forest path towards the gingerbread house of her dearest dreams and, more importantly, the oven contained within.

Given the nature of impresarios and their desire to stay out of the spotlight as much as possible, everything that Leonarda had conveyed made perfect sense. Such a man would need an able secretary to tackle all of the hands-on workings of his businesses, and he'd be reluctant to have his name bandied around when recruiting such a secretary. Leonarda's lack of knowledge about the intricacies of what she was proposing just served to prove that she wasn't withholding information from Virginia deliberately. Every fault in her story was explained away by the secretive employer. It was perfect. Even the demands that were passed down, about not telling anyone where she was going or what she was doing, seemed entirely within the realms of possibility.

Everything was set up in exactly the same way as the previous murders, but this time, Leonarda combined the best aspects of both. She felt everything completely, so that her suffering would correctly mirror Virginia's, and she made use of all the careful preparation that had made the physical aspects of Francesca's slaying so efficient.

A promise was made, and the secret details of the travelling arrangements were delivered by mail to Leonarda, to be conveyed on the day that Virginia was due to leave, and not a moment sooner.

Virginia rose late on the 30th of September, 1940, to say goodbye to her brother and thank him for his kindness in keeping her through her penury. Her sister-in-law was already out, so there was no opportunity to say goodbye. She arrived on Leonarda's doorstep just a short while before midday, to find the soap shop closed and the bustle of her busy house silenced. It was bizarre. Even in her most private moments with Leonarda, the whole building had heaved with life. Today, it was like approaching some rickety mausoleum.

Now that she was leaving Correggio, Virginia no longer felt the need to tone herself down or hide who she was for fear of offending the locals. She was draped in furs and glittering with jewellery – the height of glamour and sophistication. Leonarda was taken aback. This was the woman that she'd always imagined Virginia to be, the woman that she'd imagined that she could've been in some other life, but now, seeing her in all her glory, it was difficult to go ahead with the plan. This wasn't some lonely widow or pathetic spinster that she was contemplating blotting out. It was a woman who'd lived the kind of illustrious life that people like Leonarda could only dream about.

Inferiority was not a feeling that sat well with Leonarda. Looking at Virginia in all of her glory may have taken her aback for a moment, but now it hardened her resolve. How could she have ever thought of this creature as her friend when Virginia had clearly been looking down on her and laughing behind her back at her quaint habits this entire time? It was a flimsy justification for the anger that she needed, but Leonarda latched onto it all the same.

She settled Virginia at her kitchen table, as she had the other two, then went to fetch a glass of wine for her from the pantry. Virginia said that it was too early in the day, that she wanted to keep a clear head for travelling. She had a dozen excuses ready before Leonarda had even emptied the sachet of poison into the crystal goblet and had given it a stir. The tinkling of the spoon on the glass was easy to hear through in the kitchen, and all of Leonarda's reasons rang just a little bit false as she cajoled Virginia into drinking it. Even to the last, Virginia was a graceful and loyal friend. 'I don't know why you're so intent on me drinking this wine, but if it is important to you, then I shall.'

The trust that she was showing in Leonarda and her strange ways would've been heart-warming if Leonarda's heart weren't already so set on its course. There was a twist of guilt that hadn't been there with the other women. They'd been tricked, but Virginia was trusting her with her life, trusting blindly that her friend was doing something to help rather than harm her. Leonarda was repaying that trust with literal poison.

As Virginia began to drift, Leonarda quietly divested her of her fine clothes and jewels. She packed it all away in her friend's trunk, then dragged that hefty thing through to join the others in storage. Her arms were tired after that, so she returned to the kitchen to consider her victim. Stripped of her finery, Virginia still looked more beautiful than Leonarda could've ever hoped to be. Her perfume still hung in the air like she was some fragrant garden, and her face, though slack and gormless, still held a grace that Leonarda's never would. She was beautiful, for now.

The axe was where Leonarda had left it, propped just inside the pantry out of sight. The trays and the pots were stowed away in cupboards, but she had them laid out in her preferred patterns in a matter of minutes. This wasn't becoming routine to her, but she'd learned her lessons well and set to the work methodically. However, she didn't let herself focus on the task at hand to the exclusion of the pain that she was feeling. Her actions couldn't be allowed to be an escape for her. She had to suffer, or it would all be for nothing.

She wondered, as she hefted the axe, whether it would've been better to see Virginia awake and aware of her end, or if this was kinder. If it was kinder, should she wait until Virginia stirred? She'd given the singer only a small dose of the sedatives because of her slighter build. It wouldn't take long for them to work their way out of her system. She was pondering what it would look like when Virginia spasmodically twitched in her sleep.

Leonarda let out a yelp and brought down the axe. It bit deep into Virginia's chest. Her ribs splintered. Her pale skin split and wept a great tide of blood. Leonarda hissed and dragged the axe back out. Virginia wouldn't spoil this. She wouldn't let her. She swung again, splitting arm from torso in a gruesome rush of red. Then, again, on the other side. Her arms ached, and each impact sent a painful shudder up to her shoulders, yet she didn't stop. She was gasping for air through her mouth once more, desperately trying to avoid the cloying scent of death and sobbing between each swing of the axe. She could smell it, despite all that — floral and charnel blending in her head.

The blood ran rich and as red as wine into the basins. The flesh, so dainty and pale on the outside, was layered with a thick, white fat beneath the surface. It was perfect. Leonarda placed each piece of flesh reverentially into the great pots on her stove and turned up the heat, watching the caustic soda eating away at the evidence before her very eyes. It wasn't right. Something about the smell set her eyes twitching. Everything had to be right.

From Virginia's trunk, she dragged out a bottle of expensive perfume, sniffing at it to be sure it was the one that her victim had been wearing today. She dumped the whole bottle into her soap-soup. That was better — the soap smelled like Virginia again. Leonarda let out a little sigh of relief. It was best to keep a lid on the soap for the rest of this process, but she could feel in her bones that it was going to work this time. She'd found the missing ingredients of the ritual.

The blood, she prepared as usual, and the teacakes soon followed after, but when Leonarda bit into them, she was startled at the flavour. They weren't dry and tinged with iron. They were sweet, far sweeter than they had any right to be. Even in death, Virginia's sweetness lived on. Leonarda couldn't have asked for a better guardian angel for her beloved son than the woman she'd once called a friend.

Where the others had handed their fortunes to Leonarda freely, this time, she felt every bit the thief when she was digging through Virginia's clothes, rifling through all that was left of her like some sort of grave robber. The 50,000 lire tucked in the bottom of the chest was more than she could hope to make in a year. There were public bonds worth almost as much stowed away in Virginia's clothing in case of emergency, and the jewels and the clothes would provide enough that she'd never have to fear the shadow of insolvency again once they were sold. Giuseppe would live. Leonarda would never struggle again. All of her problems were solved in one day, all thanks to Virginia.

This time, when the cleaning was done, and it was time to check on the soap, Leonarda felt no trepidation. She knew that she'd done everything right. She knew that the spell had been cast, just as she'd meant for it to be. The soap was rich and creamy. The aroma, sweet and floral. It was everything it was meant to be. Leonarda added her own final ingredients to the soap unintentionally — salt water. Tears, streaming unbidden down her cheeks in memory of her beloved friend. So sweet and kind that even in death she'd go on giving. Leonarda's tears dried as she formed the bars of soap, the warmth of the stovetop radiating up to wipe away any trace of them.

When all trace of her crimes was tucked away safely, the day was spent, and she knew that Giuseppe would be returning soon, she placed the pots back on the stove and set water to boil. She wasn't going to risk any delay. Tonight, he would come home, and tonight, he would eat the cakes and bathe with the soap. Every inch of his skin would be covered. There'd be no Achilles heel for her son — she'd learned from the mistakes of antiquity. There'd be no pause for him to slip through her fingers, either. The window of opportunity for fate to strike Giuseppe down was narrowing. There'd never been a more dangerous time for him. She cursed herself for letting him roam so far afield that day. He came home according to schedule, but every moment until she saw him, Leonarda's heart hammered in her chest.

Together, they pulled down the bath and filled it up. She watched him intently as he stripped down and clambered in, awkwardly trying to cover himself from his mother's stare, but it wasn't out of some prurient interest in his body. She was watching for any sign of injury, any sign that she'd taken too long or moved too slow. She could see nothing. Her boy was perfect. He'd always been perfect. It mattered little to her that he flinched away from her touch or shuddered with disgust as her hands slipped over the parts of him that he held to be private. The soap was ideal. Creamy and rich. Floral and fragrant. Everything that she could've wanted from soap.

When it was done, and Giuseppe sat by the kitchen table wrapped in a towel, refusing to look at her, she fed him teacakes. When he wouldn't eat, she picked them up and guided the food to his lips as she had when he was just a babe in swaddling.

Inside and out, he was protected. She'd done it. It was finally over. Fate couldn't harm him now. He wouldn't die before her. The spell was cast. The curse was defeated. She'd won. By skill and will, she'd overturned the universe and remade it in her own image. If there were a God above, then she'd spat in his eye and set herself above him.

Even as the days passed them by, Giuseppe still wouldn't speak or meet her eye. Her final act of protection had severed whatever connection there'd been between them. All those years of maternal love and affection sacrificed on the altar of his survival. She didn't care. Sacrifice was at the root of the magic she'd worked. If she had to cut him free of her to be safe, then that is what she had to do. Her dark fate couldn't spread to him if there were no connection for it to insinuate its way along. She'd lost her son, but if that meant that he wouldn't die as he was doomed to, it was worth it. These were all small prices to pay in comparison to the prize that she'd won.

With her life's work complete, all that Leonarda had left to do now was live out the rest of her days and dispose of what remained of Virginia. The teacakes didn't go to waste. Every day, Leonarda had a half dozen visitors that she shared advice, tea, and coffee with. She hoped that some portion of the protection spell might be passed on to them, too. As for the soap, she wouldn't tarnish the sacrifice that she'd made by selling it, but she was happy to make a gift of a bar of it here and there to those that she considered her most important friends. If the protection spell rubbed off on them, all the better. If not, it was still some perfectly serviceable soap that she didn't want to go to waste.

The evidence of her crimes vanished, bite by bite and wash by wash until there was no trace left of the women that these consumable objects had been. The letters were sent, assuaging any doubts, and the vast sums of money that Leonarda had earned were squirrelled away. She'd never been lavish in her spending and, given her complicated feelings about where the wealth had come from, she seemed loathed to touch it. Her reluctance probably saved her from quite a bit of unwanted attention. Once more, luck happened to align her fantasy world with the real world in ways that benefitted her.

Giuseppe still couldn't face his mother after she'd bathed him, but even from a distance, he could see the change in her. She moved through life without a burden heaped on her shoulders. There may have been a sad look in her eyes, but the terror and fury that had always driven her on seemed to have been snuffed out. It was another little tragedy that the woman she'd now become was probably the kind of mother that Giuseppe could've had a healthy relationship with, at last. Instead, he counted down the days until he could leave town.

An Embittered Soul's
Confessions

Matters with her victims' families weren't quite as settled as Leonarda would've liked to think. The letters had certainly calmed the initial panic at their disappearance, but when further correspondence wasn't forthcoming, concerns began to arise. Virginia's sister-in-law had been as close to her as any blood relative and had helped her through all of her later years of penury, just as she'd supported her during her time on the stage. She, at least, couldn't believe that everyone would be so accepting of this ridiculous story about a mysterious impresario that wanted to hire a stranger, who hadn't set foot in a theatre for years, to manage his businesses. Without the bait of Virginia's desperation on the hook, it did seem beyond belief. What sort of employer would demand such secrecy from a secretary? How did Virginia even get in contact with this mystery man? Why would someone in a big city choose someone banished to provincial life over women with far more experience and active contacts in the industry? There were too many questions with no satisfying answer.

Mrs Cacioppo had nothing but suspicions and letters that made little sense to explain what had happened to her beloved sister-in-law, so she began investigating matters on her own. Broaching the social strata, she started asking around about the people that her sister-in-law had been spending time with, searching for the connection to this impresario so that she could follow the links of the chain back to whoever was really behind Virginia's sudden vanishing. Correggio didn't boast much of a social scene, and Virginia's options had been limited by her budget, but even among those few people, there was nobody who had a clue what Mrs Cacioppo was talking about.

When left at a dead-end in her search, Mrs Cacioppo stopped asking who'd done it and, instead, switched tack to asking who could've done it. Leonarda's reputation preceded her. If you wanted the impossible done in Correggio, she was the one that you'd ask. If you wanted all of your dreams to come true, she was the one who could guide you to your path. Mrs Cacioppo wasn't the most romantically inclined woman in town — she'd never seen fit to avail herself of the fortune teller's services and scoffed at the women who had. Despite Leonarda's long tenure in town, their paths had never really crossed.

When she arrived at Leonarda's door with a mind full of questions, the experience that followed was confusing, to say the least. She barely managed to get a few words out before Leonarda took her by the hand and led her in for a cup of coffee and a palm reading. It was the same routine that she'd worked with every other woman in town to great effect, but the sceptical Cacioppo spent the whole time thinking about how easily a person could be manipulated by a woman like this, one who seemed to have all the answers yet could twist her own words at the drop of a hat to fit whatever narrative her victim was seeking. It was only after Leonarda had promised health and prosperity to her grandchildren that Mrs Cacioppo finally managed to turn the conversation to her sister-in-law. At once, Leonarda's whole demeanour changed. She apologised profusely but couldn't tell Cacioppo any more than she already knew. Virginia had told her about her trip, but that was all. When tears sprang to her eyes unbidden, she explained it away as missing her dear friend. Cacioppo's suspicions grew.

Quick conversations with Leonarda's neighbours soon provided Cacioppo with a timeline of Virginia's departure. This was the last place that the former soprano had been seen before vanishing without a trace. Nobody had seen her leave the building. Nobody had seen a taxi. She'd gone into Leonarda's house and never returned. Armed with this little titbit on top of her already growing suspicions, Cacioppo went to the police. The locals had already treated her worries with scorn, so she passed them over and approached the superintendent for the whole province of Reggio Emilia.

A simple investigation uncovered the disappearance of the other two women, and more thorough work began to link the vanished women to Leonarda's household. The stories of the neighbours became more tangled with the other women because it had been some time since they were last seen in Correggio, but the police were able to confirm that both of them visited Leonarda on or around the date of their disappearances.

Leonarda was brought in for questioning as the obvious point of contact between the three women, but she gave the police nothing. She was an astute liar by this time in her career as a fortune teller, able to twist and turn inflection and meaning as easily as others might draw a breath. She admitted to knowing all three of the missing women and to advising them in their affairs, but she certainly didn't know anything about their disappearances. She probably had seen them before they left town, but most women sought out her counsel before setting off on a long journey – there wasn't any deeper significance to it beyond her own importance.

The police investigation didn't stop just because she was stonewalling them. They didn't have the evidence they needed to meet Italy's strict demands for search and seizure of private property, so they had to expand their work elsewhere. Every available piece of evidence was methodically worked back until it could be connected to Leonarda. The letters were the only physical evidence that the police had to work with, but by examining the envelopes and calculating delivery times, they were able to track the specific dates that the three of them had been sent. From there, they followed the postmarks to the local post offices and interviewed around until they found out who'd sent them. They were expecting Leonarda, but what they got was Guiseppe. It took them a little while to connect the description of a young man with Leonarda's eldest son, but when they did, a whole new picture snapped into place.

The focus of the investigation shifted to him, and with that latest piece of evidence, there was enough to raid the soap shop and house. Stowed away in a closet, they found all of the belongings of the missing women that Leonarda hadn't yet managed to sell along: a chest containing all of the money and public bonds and a few pieces of jewellery that had been made to order for Virginia. What had started as suspicion had now taken a considerably darker turn.

The money provided more than ample motive, and it seemed entirely possible that young Giuseppe, whom everyone knew had plans to leave town soon, had killed those women as a means to acquire his fresh start. The narrative made considerably more sense than some nonsense about an old fortune-teller killing people, and the police were relieved to bring in their suspect.

Giuseppe was of no use to the police whatsoever. He was completely unable to answer the fundamental question that would transform this from a case of missing people into a murder investigation: Where were the bodies? But neither Giuseppe nor any of the investigators had been able to answer that question. These women hadn't just gone missing; they'd vanished. The clothing that two of the women had been wearing was found among their recovered belongings, and there was no possibility that a pair of nude women roaming the streets of Correggio could've gone unnoticed. Nobody was even considering the possibility that they were alive anymore. All that the police had to do now was lean on the boy until he came clean about his murderous schemes.

What nobody had counted on was the suspect's mother showing up at the police station, banging on the door just a few hours later, ready to make a full confession to the crimes her son stood accused of. The police were happy to interview her again, even if it was with an air of bemusement at this old woman trying to take her son's place on the chopping block. It was sweet, really, the kind of thing that they could all imagine their dear mothers trying to do for them if they ever got into trouble. They went right on treating her as an adorable joke until the moment she started to describe her murders in grotesque detail. By the time that she'd recounted how she poisoned and chopped up her three victims, the police were no longer smiling. Her story had contained details that only someone who'd witnessed a murder might know. They now considered her to be an accessory to the murder.

What mother wouldn't have tried to cover up her son's crimes? All that they really needed from her so-called confession was the answer to where the bodies were buried, which was when the investigation finally took another dark turn towards the truth. She told them, in detail, about the way that she drained off the blood and dried it in the oven. The police weren't familiar with caustic soda any more than Giuseppe was, so she had to tell them all about the effects of the compound in agonising detail before they could grasp that they weren't going to be finding any bodies. She'd liquified her victims and poured them out like yesterday's leftovers, all except for her beloved Virginia, who'd made the perfect soap.

The police were all looking queasy as they recounted this story to Giuseppe, hoping against hope that he'd provide them with some other story that they could pretend was the truth. Instead, they had to watch as all of the colour drained from his face, and he began vomiting. The bizarre bathtime ritual suddenly made sense, and all of the secrets about his mother that he'd been holding back poured out in a great nauseous wave. He told them about her study, the curse, and her occult obsessions. Everything that he knew, he told them, not to buy his freedom, but to free himself from the guilt of knowing that such horrors had happened in his very own home.

Leonarda felt no such compunctions. She didn't feel guilt, shame, or even disgust in her actions anymore. They'd been necessary to protect Giuseppe from the laws of the universe, just as her own sacrifice now was necessary to protect him from the laws of man. Everything that she'd done, she did out of love. Everything that she was, she would gleefully surrender, so long as her son was safe. There could be no higher calling for a mother.

While, until now, the police interviewing her had been sympathetic, they now shied away from her. The image of the kindly mother doing anything for her son had been shattered. Now they looked upon her like she was an ogre from a fairy tale. There were rumours of witchcraft and Satanism rippling out through the town, and before too long, every tongue in Correggio was wagging with tales of the wicked witch whom they'd known was up to no good all along. Every piece of advice that she'd given was reconsidered in light of these new sinister suspicions. Her whole legacy as the guide and guardian of Correggio's womenfolk was dissolved in a single day. She didn't care a jot. Her task was complete, the curse was defeated, and all that she felt was pride.

The Pansardi family were shunned from the moment that Leonarda made her confession, and when tales of cannibalism and humans turned into soap began to spread, their soap business immediately went under. None of the money that she'd stolen from her victims was leftover, and her children were so horrified at the monster that had birthed them that they scattered to the winds. Everything that Leonarda had worked for disappeared. Raffaele remained like a ghost of her former life, but he, too, was broken by the knowledge that the woman he loved was capable of such monstrous acts. He tried to behave as a husband should, supporting and loving Leonarda in the run-up to her trial, but he just didn't have the words. He stayed because he had nowhere else to go, but he had nothing to say.

Giuseppe's military deployment was a welcome relief to the boy. He'd wanted to escape his mother's shadow before all of this came to light, and now the very weight of her name was crushing. He would've gone to hell itself rather than remain in her reach. He left Italy with his unit, never even considering stopping by the jailhouse to say goodbye. The uncomfortable experience of being bathed by his mother would've been enough to destroy their relationship — this was just another nail in the coffin.

The case took years to build and even longer to bring to court with the chaos of the Second World War still in full swing. The pots, basins, trays, and axes that she'd used in the disposal of the bodies were all laid out on the bench before her, and she identified them and their uses. The only thing that was missing was a copper ladle that she'd used to skim the fat off the top of the pots as the caustic soda dissolved her victims. When asked where it had gone, she announced that she'd donated the metal to the war effort.

Even now, in the dock for murder, she was a proud and patriotic Italian, and she expected to receive praise. Her fantasy world had always governed her reality, but now, for the first time, she was being confronted with an inflexible world where how she felt she should be seen wasn't reflected in the eyes of others. The judge wasn't impressed by her patriotism any more than the crowds were impressed with her quasi-mystical justifications for murder. It rankled Leonarda. She'd been almost perpetually alone for the last six years, transferred from jails to holding cells and back again before finally arriving in Reggio Emelia, and this was meant to be her moment in the spotlight. She'd spent so long hiding from the eyes of the world, and now she finally had the chance to show everyone what kind of person she was.

Leonarda narrated the full list of her crimes. She was completely cold-blooded in her description of the gruesome events, and she was lavish with the details. It went beyond the point of painting a realistic picture and over the edge into prurient delight. Every time that she saw the family members of her victims pale or flinch, it seemed to give her energy. When her ex-neighbours doubted the story that she was telling could be true, she laughed in their faces. 'If I lift up my skirt and wipe your eyes, maybe then you'll see clearly.'

As her testimony rolled on, she started bandying about bawdy jokes. The whole court was silent except for her braying laughter. When others were speaking, she would interrupt to butt in with some inane fact or another about her crimes or her areas of dubious expertise. She became more and more histrionic, cackling and spitting. Being the centre of attention was her long-unfulfilled dream, and she couldn't stand for the spotlight to shine on anyone else.

From the cold, calculating description of her first day in court to the second and third, there was a marked degeneration as her emotions bled into her testimony. The fierce joy that she'd taken in killing began to creep in, honesty, at last, overwhelming the layers of fantasy and self-deception that she'd wrapped around herself to maintain her sanity. Now that she was being seen, she began to unravel.

An expert witness was brought out to discuss the method that she'd used to dispose of the bodies, a coroner with experience in acids. He claimed that a body couldn't be destroyed with caustic soda in the way that Leonarda had described. Leonarda was enraged. 'Bring a body to court. Give me a body of any age, right now, and I shall prove it.'

She was muffled and dragged off before she could threaten the coroner personally, but her point was well made. The one person in the world with the most experience in the subject of caustic soda body disposal was standing trial for making use of that expertise.

After six years of waiting, Leonarda was convicted in only three days. She'd convinced everyone in the court that she was the homicidal maniac in her family and washed away any doubts in a flood of bloody description. She'd also convinced the court that she'd committed her crimes because she was profoundly mentally ill.

Her sentence was 30 years in prison, followed by a three-year stint in a mental asylum to ensure that she was safe to return to society. The prophecy that she'd received as a young woman was coming true at last: in one hand prison, in the other, the asylum.

The Ultimate Fate

Pozzuoli Prison was to be Leonarda's home for the coming decades. She'd spent time in prison before, but this time, she wasn't bathed in shame and trying to pretend that she wasn't there, nor was she confined in some pseudo-religious institution for 'naughty girls.' Pozzuoli was a converted men's prison, under the normal remit of the Ministry of the Interior rather than a nunnery gone awry. There were rules in place that governed the care that prisoners received and the standards by which they could be judged. Compared to the harsh life that Leonarda and many of the other women around her had endured, this prison was a welcome relief — a place where they didn't have to work themselves to the bone just to survive. For Leonarda, this felt like her reward. She'd done what she needed to do, and now she could retire in the lap of relative luxury, seen for the first time not just as someone's wife or a guiding star for someone else's journey through life, but as herself. Completely honest and open.

This new Leonarda proved to be particularly popular among the other women of Pozzuoli. She arrived riding a wave of national fame and received a standing ovation on arrival. Pride of place in the complex hierarchy of the prison was reserved for her, and she settled in comfortably.

Hard labour had never been on the cards for an older woman like her, but everyone was expected to take on some tasks to ensure the maintenance of the prison itself. With her skills, Leonarda soon found a place for herself in the kitchens. Outside of the huge batch meals that she cooked for everyone in the building, she began baking for her sister inmates, and they were delighted by the little treats that she produced. She was more than happy to share with anyone, but for some reason, the guards couldn't be tempted to try any of the many snacks that she made, despite all of the widespread praise that they received.

Even with her time spent primarily in the kitchen, Leonarda still found the long evenings stretching out ahead of her in her cell. Here, she held court as late as she dared, chatting away with the other women, offering them advice on their troubles just as she had the women of Correggio, but after a certain point, the guards would come by and drive off her attendants, leaving her bored and alone. It was then that inspiration struck. Her day in court had taught Leonarda how much she enjoyed being the centre of attention, and there'd been no shortage of psychiatrists interested in prying the secrets out of her since her confinement. She didn't trust doctors, and she didn't trust anyone else to tell her tale. It was important to her that she be seen in her entirety, not just as a mish-mash of symptoms and syndromes. So it was, that she committed herself to write an autobiography, from which many of the confirmed details in this very book were drawn.

She titled her book The Confessions of an Embittered Soul, and it followed through her entire life story, starting with the rape of her mother and carrying on through her abusive upbringing, suicide attempts, and on into adulthood and her obsession with the occult. There were a great many stories contained within the book that couldn't be substantiated — tales of the many seductions that she'd performed throughout the years and her sexual voracity. If she was to be believed, then half of the population of rural Italy had slept with her at one point or another; the husbands of all her many friends and many of those women, too. It seems plausible that she furnished her book with the latter titillating detail after taking a lover while serving her prison sentence, but she didn't seem to favour any one woman among her inner circle of confidants across her 30 years in jail.

She also filled her book with recipes, pouring all of her knowledge of cookery onto the page alongside gruesome descriptions of the way that she'd dismembered the corpses of her victims and reduced them to a gory pulp. Even the cannibalistic teacake recipe was included in this book, minus the blood, right alongside the depiction of her draining her victims. Bizarrely, this book was one of the most complete collections of traditional Italian baking techniques ever written, and it's still referred to by some of the top chefs of Italy today.

It was 20 years into her sentence that Leonarda suffered what seemed at the time to be a minor stroke. She was a hearty woman, and she recovered from it quickly, but symptoms kept on recurring until eventually, a doctor realised that she had an ongoing bleed within her brain. They couldn't understand the cause of this issue. She'd suffered from epileptic seizures throughout her life, induced by stress and originally presumed to have been caused by some sort of traumatic head injury at the hands of her mother that she'd lost all recollection of, but that didn't explain the bleeding. It was only when reviewing Leonarda's case notes that the doctors realised the cause — caustic soda vapour poisoning. The same material that she'd used to eat through her victims' flesh had burrowed holes through her brain, something like poetic justice.

This intracranial bleeding went on throughout the years, causing Leonarda's sight and faculties to fail her, and setting off a recurrence of the seizures that had plagued her through her younger life. By the time that her 30-year prison sentence was over and she was transferred into the medical care of an asylum, she actually needed to be there for support as much as assessment.

Little of the records from her time there have survived the years, but a great many doctors made wildly varying diagnoses of the root cause of her homicidal actions and bizarre anxiety disorders. All of them agreed that her relationship with her mother was the root cause of her behaviours, but nobody could seem to agree on a single diagnosis beyond that point. It was generally assumed that some strange combination of mental illnesses and external pressures had combined to create her particular murderous fantasies, but there didn't seem to be any terminology for it. Even with hindsight and the full breadth of her writings to study, psychiatrists today struggle to identify exactly what kind of monster Leonarda Cianciulli was, although it certainly seems likely that she'd score well on modern tests for psychopathy.

On the 14th of October, 1970, just a year before she was due to be released, the pressure of too much blood building up inside her skull drove Leonarda into a coma, and just a day later, her intracranial bleeding finally killed her. Her mind was flooded with blood for so long, with nowhere for it to escape to, that it eventually crushed every part of her that was thinking and alive. Her official cause of death was given as 'cerebral apoplexy.' There was no aggravating factor to cause her death, no outside cause, or particular stress. She was 76 years old, living as comfortable a life as she ever had and still joking with the orderlies and inmates up until the very last moment before she dropped. It was as though fate had just chosen to strike her down before she could walk free.

Her family couldn't be contacted to claim her remains following her death and, wanting no grave to be desecrated, the Italian authorities secretly cremated and disposed of her remains. After her death, many of her belongings were donated to the Criminology Museum in Rome, including the pots and axes that she used in her murders. Her 'Confessions' have been published several times over by small presses trying to make the most of her latest round of notoriety, and several films and plays have been written that reflected the details of Leonarda's crimes — most famously the 1977 film 'Gran Bollito' and the 1983 Broadway play 'Love and Magic in Mama's Kitchen'.

One prophecy had been fulfilled. Leonarda had been confined in both prison and asylum before she finally expired, but the other prophecy that was given to her all those years ago, when she'd first gone seeking answers to her mother's curse, still hung over her — the promise that every one of her children would die before her.

For obvious reasons, every one of her surviving children went through a period of hiding after the trial began, and Leonarda Pansardi became a household name. Raffaele Pansardi certainly died before Leonarda, many miles to the south in somewhere even more rural than the villages they'd lived in before. He was dead before she'd even stood trial, drinking away his troubles until his heart gave out.

Changing your name in circumstances outside of a new marriage was possible under Italian law, but it created something of a paper trail, allowing anyone to access the public documents and confirm your original identity. For this reason, it seems likely that the change in name that the children enacted was more informal. Her two younger children scattered to the winds, went by different names, married, and settled in distant places where the ghost of their mother could no longer loom over them. The massive registration of identities that nation-states would undertake in the 20th century was underway by this point, but in the chaotic years following the war, so much information was lost, found, and muddled beyond all recognition. There was no better time for them to slip through the cracks.

As for Giuseppe himself, there is a record of his deployment to the African theatre, and it seems more than likely that he was redirected as the Italian forces fought their retreat from their imperial holdings in East Africa into the Tunisia campaign. There, the Italian and German forces won several key victories that seemed to be turning the tide of war in their favour before interdiction tactics cut off their supply lines and left them without the supplies that they needed to continue. In May 1943, the Afrika Korps was brought to its knees, and while some of their leadership escaped, the vast majority of the Italian 1st Army was captured by the Allied forces and transported back to the UK as prisoners of war. It would be here that any official record of Giuseppe Pansardi would be likely to appear, but his name is nowhere to be seen. Either he died in the fields of Africa, or he had successfully passed himself off as someone else, to the degree that even the military of his own country had been fooled when preparing his papers.

Leonarda's sacrifices had all been in vain. Even if she'd protected Giuseppe from death, she'd instilled in him such a horror of her that he'd scratched her name off his own. Dead or alive, she'd lost him.

THE CURSE

About the Author

Ryan Green is a true crime author in his late thirties. He lives in Herefordshire, England with his wife, three children, and two dogs. Outside of writing and spending time with his family, Ryan enjoys walking, reading and windsurfing.

Ryan is fascinated with History, Psychology and True Crime. In 2015, he finally started researching and writing his own work and at the end of the year, he released his first book on Britain's most notorious serial killer, Harold Shipman.

He has since written several books on lesser-known subjects, and taken the unique approach of writing from the killer's perspective. He narrates some of the most chilling scenes you'll encounter in the True Crime genre.

You can sign up to Ryan's newsletter to receive a free book, updates, and the latest releases at:

WWW.RYANGREENBOOKS.COM

More Books by Ryan Green

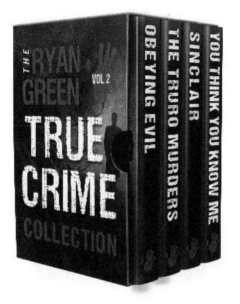

4 books for the price of 2 (save 50%)

Four chilling true crime stories in one collection, from the bestselling author Ryan Green.

Volume 2 contains some of Green's most fascinating accounts of violence, abuse, deception and murder. Within this collection, you'll receive:

- Obeying Evil
- The Truro Murders
- Sinclair
- You Think You Know Me

More Books by Ryan Green

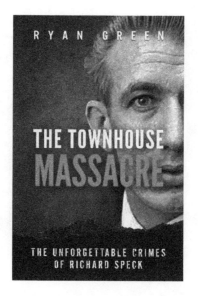

"It just wasn't their night" – Richard Speck

On the evening of 13 July 1966, an intoxicated Richard Speck broke into a townhouse at 2319 East 100th Street in Chicago, to rob a group of student nurses. Speck woke the residents and ordered them into a room, calmly requesting money in exchange for their safety. The young women obliged. They believed that he was just going to take the money and leave but Speck had other plans.

He tied them all up with strips of bed linen, and led one of the girls into a separate room to "talk alone". The situation took a turn for the worse when two more resident nurses burst into the townhouse, surprising Speck in the act. What transpired in the following hours would grip the nation with fear and forever change the perception of society.

More Books by Ryan Green

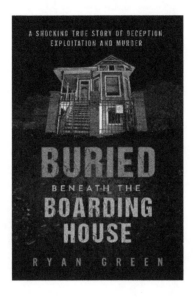

In 1988, detectives from the Sacramento Police Department were called to investigate the disappearance of a man at his last known address, a boarding house for the elderly, homeless and mentally ill. The owner, Dorothea Puente, was an adorable old lady who cared for stray cats and the rest of society's castaways. She had a strong standing in the community and was celebrated for her selfless charitable work.

The search revealed nothing untoward but one of the guests recalled some unusual incidents leading up to the disappearance. He shared stories about holes being dug in the garden and filled in overnight. Guests who were taken ill and vanished overnight, and a number of excuses why they couldn't be contacted. This was enough to launch a thorough investigation and on 11th November 1988, the Sacramento Police Department headed back to the boarding house with shovels in hand.

Were they wasting their time pursuing a charming and charitable old lady or were they closing in on a clandestine killer who exploited the most vulnerable members of society? The investigation gripped the entire nation and the answers lay *Buried Beneath the Boarding House.*

Free True Crime Audiobook

Listen to four chilling True Crime stories in one collection. Follow the link below to download a FREE copy of *The Ryan Green True Crime Collection: Vol. 3*.

WWW.RYANGREENBOOKS.COM/FREE-AUDIOBOOK

"Ryan Green has produced another excellent book and belongs at the top with true crime writers such as M. William Phelps, Gregg Olsen and Ann Rule" –**B.S. Reid**

"Wow! Chilling, shocking and totally riveting! I'm not going to sleep well after listening to this but the narration was fantastic. Crazy story but highly recommend for any true crime lover!" –**Mandy**

"Torture Mom by Ryan Green left me pretty speechless. The fact that it's a true story is just...wow" –**JStep**

"Graphic, upsetting, but superbly read and written" –**Ray C**

WWW.RYANGREENBOOKS.COM/FREE-AUDIOBOOK